Poems & Prose Sketches by Jam<

Poet and author James Whitcomb Riley was born on Octobei
known as the "Hoosier Poet" for his work with regional diale
Riley was born into an influential and well off family.

However his education was spotty but he was surrounded by
good stead later in life.

His early career was a series of low paid temporary jobs. After stints as a journalist and billboard
proprietor he had the resources to dedicate more of his efforts to writing.

Riley was prone to drink which was to affect his health and later his career but after a slow start and
a lot of submissions he began to gain traction first in newspapers and then with the publication of
his dialect poems 'Boone County Poems' he came to national recognition. This propelled him to long
term contracts to perform on speaking circuits. These were very successful but over the years his
star waned.

In 1888 he was too drunk to perform and the ensuing publicity made everything seem very bleak for
a while. However he overcame that and managed to re-negotiate his contracts so that he received
his rightful share of the income and his wealth thereafter increased very quickly.

A bachelor, Riley seems to have his writings as his only outlet, and although in his public
performances he was well received, his publications were becoming seen as banal and repetitive and
sales of these later works began to fall away.

Eventually after his last tour in 1895 he retired to spend his final years in Indianapolis writing
patriotic poetry.

Now in poor health, weakened by years of heavy drinking, Riley, the Hoosier Poet died on July 23,
1916 of a stroke. In a final, unusual tribute, Riley lay in state for a day in the Indiana Statehouse,
where thousands came to pay their respects. Not since Lincoln had a public personage received such
a send-off. He is buried at Crown Hill Cemetery in Indianapolis.

Index Of Poems

James Whitcomb riley – A Short Biography

Since we have had no stories to-night I will venture, Mr. President, to tell a story that I have heretofore heard at nearly all the banquets I have ever attended. It is a story simply, and you must bear with it kindly. It is a story as told by a friend of us all, who is found in all parts of all countries, who is immoderately fond of a funny story, and who, unfortunately, attempts to tell a funny story himself, one that he has been particularly delighted with. Well, he is not a story-teller, and especially he is not a funny story-teller. His funny stories, indeed, are oftentimes touchingly pathetic. But to such a story as he tells, being a good-natured man and kindly disposed, we have to listen, because we do not want to wound his feelings by telling him that we have heard that story a great number of times, and that we have heard it ably told by a great number of people from the time we were children. But, as I say, we can not hurt his feelings. We can not stop him. We can not kill him; and so the story generally proceeds. He selects a very old story always, and generally tells it in about this fashion:

I heerd an awful funny thing the other day, ha! ha! I don't know whether I kin git it off er not, but, anyhow, I'll tell it to you. Well! le's see now how the fool-thing goes. Oh, yes! W'y, there was a feller one time, it was durin' the army, and this feller that I started in to tell you about was in the war, and, ha! ha! there was a big fight a-goin' on, and this feller was in the fight, and it was a big battle and bullets a-flyin' ever' which way, and bombshells a-bu'stin', and cannon-balls a-flyin' 'round promiskus; and this feller right in the midst of it, you know, and all excited and het up, and chargin' away; and the fust thing you know along come a cannon-ball and shot his head off, ha! ha! ha! Hold on here a minute! no sir; I'm a-gittin' ahead of my story; no, no; it didn't shoot his head off, I'm gittin' the cart before the horse there, shot his leg off; that was the way; shot his leg off; and down the poor feller drapped, and, of course, in that condition was perfectly he'pless, you know, but yit with presence o' mind enough to know that he was in a dangerous condition ef somepin' wasn't done fer him right away. So he seen a comrade a-chargin' by that he knowed, and he hollers to him and called him by name, I disremember now what the feller's name was....

Well, that's got nothin' to do with the story, anyway; he hollers to him, he did, and says, "Hello, there," he says to him; "here, I want you to come here and give me a lift; I got my leg shot off, and I want you to pack me back to the rear of the battle", where the doctors always is, you know, during a fight, and he says, "I want you to pack me back there where I can get med-dy-cinal attention er I'm a dead man, fer I got my leg shot off," he says, "and I want you to pack me back there so's the surgeons kin take keer of me." Well, the feller, as luck would have it, ricko-nized him and run to him and throwed down his own musket, so's he could pick him up; and he stooped down and picked him up and kindo' half-way shouldered him and half-way helt him betwixt his arms like, and then he turned and started back with him, ha! ha! ha! Now, mind, the fight was still a-goin' on, and right at the hot of the fight, and the feller, all excited, you know, like he was, and the soldier that had his leg shot off gittin' kindo fainty like, and his head kindo' stuck back over the feller's shoulder that was carryin' him. And he hadn't got more'n a couple o' rods with him when another cannon-ball come along and tuk his head off, shore enough! and the curious thing about it was, ha! ha! that the feller was a-packin' him didn't know that he had been hit ag'in at all, and back he went, still carryin' the deceased back, ha! ha! ha! to where the doctors could take keer of him, as he thought. Well, his cap'n happened to see him, and he thought it was a ruther cur'ous p'ceedin's, a soldier carryin' a dead body out o' the fight, don't you see? And so he hollers at him, and he says to the soldier, the cap'n did, he says, "Hullo, there; where you goin' with that thing?" the cap'n said to the soldier who was a-carryin' away the feller that had his leg shot off. Well, his head, too, by that time. So he says, "Where you goin' with that thing?" the cap'n said to the soldier who was a-carryin' away the feller that had his leg shot off. Well, the soldier he stopped, kinder halted, you know, like a private soldier will when his presidin' officer speaks to him, and he says to him, "W'y," he says, "Cap, it's a comrade o' mine and the pore feller has got his leg shot off, and I'm a-packin' him back to where the doctors is; and there was nobody to he'p him, and the feller would 'a' died in his tracks, er track ruther, if it hadn't a-been fer me, and I'm a-packin' him back where the surgeons can take keer of him; where he can get medical attendance, er his wife's a widder!" he says, "'cause he's got his leg shot off!" Then Cap'n says, "You blame fool you, he's got his head shot off." So then the feller slacked his grip on the body and let it slide down to the ground, and looked at it a minute, all puzzled, you know, and says, "W'y, he told me it was his leg!" Ha! ha! ha!

SOMEP'N COMMON-LIKE

Somep'n 'at's common-like, and good
And plain, and easy understood;
Somep'n 'at folks like me and you
Kin understand, and relish, too,
And find some sermint in 'at hits
The spot, and sticks and benefits.

We don't need nothin' extry fine;
'Cause, take the run o' minds like mine,
And we'll go more on good horse-sense
Than all your flowery eloquence;
And we'll jedge best of honest acts
By Nature's statement of the facts.

So when you're wantin' to express
Your misery, er happiness,
Er anything 'at's wuth the time
O' telling in plain talk er rhyme
Jes' sort o' let your subject run
As ef the Lord wuz listenun.

MONSIEUR LE SECRETAIRE
[JOHN CLARK RIDPATH]

Mon cher Monsieur le Secretaire,
Your song flits with me everywhere;
It lights on Fancy's prow and sings
Me on divinest voyagings:
And when my ruler love would fain
Be laid upon it high again
It mounts, and hugs itself from me
With rapturous wings still dwindlingly
On! on! till but a ghost is there
Of song, Monsieur le Secretaire!

A PHANTOM
Little baby, you have wandered far away,

And your fairy face comes back to me to-day,
But I can not feel the strands
Of your tresses, nor the play
Of the dainty velvet-touches of your hands.

Little baby, you were mine to hug and hold;
Now your arms cling not about me as of old
O my dream of rest come true,
And my richer wealth than gold,
And the surest hope of Heaven that I knew!

O for the lisp long silent, and the tone
Of merriment once mingled with my own
For the laughter of your lips,
And the kisses plucked and thrown
In the lavish wastings of your finger-tips!

Little baby, O as then, come back to me,
And be again just as you used to be,
For this phantom of you stands
All too cold and silently,
And will not kiss nor touch me with its hands.

IN THE CORRIDOR

Ah! at last alone, love!
Now the band may play
Till its sweetest tone, love,
Swoons and dies away!
They who most will miss us
We're not caring for
Who of them could kiss us
In the corridor?

Had we only known, dear,
Ere this long delay,
Just how all alone, dear,
We might waltz away,
Then for hours, like this, love,
We are longing for,
We'd have still to kiss, love,
In the corridor!

Nestle in my heart, love;
Hug and hold me close
Time will come to part, love,
Ere a fellow knows;
There! the Strauss is ended
Whirl across the floor:
Isn't waltzing splendid

In the corridor?

Louella Wainie! where are you?
Do you not hear me as I cry?
Dusk is falling; I feel the dew;
And the dark will be here by and by:
I hear no thing but the owl's hoo-hoo!
Louella Wainie! where are you?

Hand in hand to the pasture bars
We came loitering, Lou and I,
Long ere the fireflies coaxed the stars
Out of their hiding-place on high.
O how sadly the cattle moo!
Louella Wainie! where are you?

Laughingly we parted here
"I will go this way," said she,
"And you will go that way, my dear"
Kissing her dainty hand at me
And the hazels hid her from my view.
Louella Wainie! where are you?

Is there ever a sadder thing
Than to stand on the farther brink
Of twilight, hearing the marsh-frogs sing?
Nothing could sadder be, I think!
And ah! how the night-fog chills one through.
Louella Wainie! where are you?

Water-lilies and oozy leaves
Lazy bubbles that bulge and stare
Up at the moon through the gloom it weaves
Out of the willows waving there!
Is it despair I am wading through?
Louella Wainie! where are you?

Louella Wainie, listen to me,
Listen, and send me some reply,
For so will I call unceasingly
Till death shall answer me by and by
Answer, and help me to find you too!
Louella Wainie! where are you?

THE TEXT
The text: Love thou thy fellow man!

He may have sinned; One proof indeed,
He is thy fellow, reach thy hand
And help him in his need!

Love thou thy fellow man. He may
Have wronged thee then, the less excuse
Thou hast for wronging him. Obey
What he has dared refuse!

Love thou thy fellow man for, be
His life a light or heavy load,
No less he needs the love of thee
To help him on his road.

WILLIAM BROWN

"He bore the name of William Brown"
His name, at least, did not go down
With him that day
He went the way
Of certain death where duty lay.

He looked his fate full in the face
He saw his watery resting-place
Undaunted, and
With firmer hand
Held others' hopes in sure command.

The hopes of full three hundred lives
Aye, babes unborn, and promised wives!
"The odds are dread,"
He must have said,
"Here, God, is one poor life instead."

No time for praying overmuch
No time for tears, or woman's touch
Of tenderness,
Or child's caress
His last "God bless them!" stopped at "bless"

Thus man and engine, nerved with steel,
Clasped iron hands for woe or weal,
And so went down
Where dark waves drown
All but the name of William Brown.

WHY

Why are they written, all these lovers' rhymes?

I catch faint perfumes of the blossoms white
That maidens drape their tresses with at night,
And, through dim smiles of beauty and the din
Of the musicians' harp and violin,
I hear, enwound and blended with the dance,
The voice whose echo is this utterance,
Why are they written, all these lovers' rhymes?

Why are they written, all these lovers' rhymes?
I see but vacant windows, curtained o'er
With webs whose architects forevermore
Race up and down their slender threads to bind
The buzzing fly's wings whirless, and to wind
The living victim in his winding sheet.
I shudder, and with whispering lips repeat,
Why are they written, all these lovers' rhymes?

Why are they written, all these lovers' rhymes?
What will you have for answer? Shall I say
That he who sings the merriest roundelay
Hath neither joy nor hope? and he who sings
The lightest, sweetest, tenderest of things
But utters moan on moan of keenest pain,
So aches his heart to ask and ask in vain,
Why are they written,all these lovers' rhymes?

THE TOUCH OF LOVING HANDS - IMITATED

Light falls the rain-drop on the fallen leaf,
And light o'er harvest-plain and garnered sheaf
But lightlier falls the touch of loving hands.

Light falls the dusk of mild midsummer night,
And light the first star's faltering lance of light
On glimmering lawns, but lightlier loving hands.

And light the feathery flake of early snows,
Or wisp of thistle-down that no wind blows,
And light the dew, but lightlier loving hands.

Light-falling dusk, or dew, or summer rain,
Or down of snow or thistle all are vain,
Far lightlier falls the touch of loving hands.

A TEST

'Twas a test I designed, in a quiet conceit
Of myself, and the thoroughly fixed and complete
Satisfaction I felt in the utter control

Of the guileless young heart of the girl of my soul.

So we parted. I said it were better we should
That she could forget me, I knew that she could;
For I never was worthy so tender a heart,
And so for her sake it were better to part.

She averted her gaze, and she sighed and looked sad
As I held out my hand for the ring that she had
With the bitterer speech that I hoped she might be
Resigned to look up and be happy with me.

'Twas a test, as I said but God pity your grief,
At a moment like this when a smile of relief
Shall leap to the lips of the woman you prize,
And no mist of distress in her glorious eyes.

A SONG FOR CHRISTMAS

Chant me a rhyme of Christmas
Sing me a jovial song,
And though it is filled with laughter,
Let it be pure and strong.

Let it be clear and ringing,
And though it mirthful be,
Let a low, sweet voice of pathos
Run through the melody.

Sing of the hearts brimmed over
With the story of the day
Of the echo of childish voices
That will not die away.

Of the blare of the tasselled bugle,
And the timeless clatter and beat
Of the drum that throbs to muster
Squadrons of scampering feet.

Of the wide-eyed look of wonder,
And the gurgle of baby-glee,
As the infant hero wrestles
From the smiling father's knee.

Sing the delights unbounded
Of the home unknown of care,
Where wealth as a guest abideth,
And want is a stranger there.

But O let your voice fall fainter,

Till, blent with a minor tone,
You temper your song with the beauty
Of the pity Christ hath shown:

And sing one verse for the voiceless;
And yet, ere the song be done,
A verse for the ears that hear not,
And a verse for the sightless one:

And one for the outcast mother,
And one for the sin-defiled
And hopeless sick man dying,
And one for his starving child.

For though it be time for singing
A merry Christmas glee,
Let a low, sweet voice of pathos
Run through the melody.

SUN AND RAIN

All day the sun and rain have been as friends,
Each vying with the other which shall be
Most generous in dowering earth and sea
With their glad wealth, till each, as it descends,
Is mingled with the other, where it blends
In one warm, glimmering mist that falls on me
As once God's smile fell over Galilee.
The lily-cup, filled with it, droops and bends
Like some white saint beside a sylvan shrine
In silent prayer; the roses at my feet,
Baptized with it as with a crimson wine,
Gleam radiant in grasses grown so sweet,
The blossoms lift, with tenderness divine,
Their wet eyes heavenward with these of mine.

WITH HER FACE

With her face between his hands!
Was it any wonder she
Stood atiptoe tremblingly?
As his lips along the strands
Of her hair went lavishing
Tides of kisses, such as swing
Love's arms to like iron bands.
With her face between his hands!

And the hands, the hands that pressed
The glad face. Ah! where are they?

Folded limp, and laid away
Idly over idle breast?
He whose kisses drenched her hair,
As he caught and held her there,
In Love's alien, lost lands,
With her face between his hands?

Was it long and long ago,
When her face was not as now,
Dim with tears? nor wan her brow
As a winter-night of snow?
Nay, anointing still the strands
Of her hair, his kisses flow
Flood-wise, as she dreaming stands,
With her face between his hands.

MY NIGHT

Hush! hush! list, heart of mine, and hearken low!
You do not guess how tender is the Night,
And in what faintest murmurs of delight
Her deep, dim-throated utterances flow
Across the memories of long-ago!
Hark! do your senses catch the exquisite
Staccatos of a bird that dreams he sings?
Nay, then, you hear not rightly, 'tis a blur
Of misty love-notes, laughs and whisperings
The Night pours o'er the lips that fondle her,
And that faint breeze, filled with all fragrant sighs,
That is her breath that quavers lover-wise
O blessed sweetheart, with thy swart, sweet kiss,
Baptize me, drown me in black swirls of bliss!

THE HOUR BEFORE THE DAWN

The hour before the dawn!
O ye who grope therein, with fear and dread
And agony of soul, be comforted,
Knowing, ere long, the darkness will be gone,
And down its dusky aisles the light be shed;
Therefore, in utter trust, fare on, fare on,
This hour before the dawn!

GOOD-BY, OLD YEAR

Good-by, Old Year!
Good-by!
We have been happy, you and I;

We have been glad in many ways;
And now, that you have come to die,
Remembering our happy days,
'Tis hard to say, "Good-by
Good-by, Old Year!
Good-by!"

Good-by, Old Year!
Good-by!
We have seen sorrow, you and I
Such hopeless sorrow, grief and care,
That now, that you have come to die,
Remembering our old despair,
'Tis sweet to say, "Good-by
Good-by, Old Year!
Good-by!"

FALSE AND TRUE

One said: "Here is my hand to lean upon
As long as you may need it." And one said:
"Believe me true to you till I am dead."
And one, whose dainty way it was to fawn
About my face, with mellow fingers drawn
Most soothingly o'er brow and drooping head,
Sighed tremulously: "Till my breath is fled
Know I am faithful!" ... Now, all these are gone
And many like to them and yet I make
No bitter moan above their grassy graves
Alas! they are not dead for me to take
Such sorry comfort! but my heart behaves
Most graciously, since one who never spake
A vow is true to me for true love's sake.

A BALLAD FROM APRIL

I am dazed and bewildered with living
A life but an intricate skein
Of hopes and despairs and thanksgiving
Wound up and unravelled again
Till it seems, whether waking or sleeping,
I am wondering ever the while
At a something that smiles when I'm weeping,
And a something that weeps when I smile.

And I walk through the world as one dreaming
Who knows not the night from the day,
For I look on the stars that are gleaming,
And lo, they have vanished away:

And I look on the sweet-summer daylight,
And e'en as I gaze it is fled,
And, veiled in a cold, misty, gray light,
The winter is there in its stead.

I feel in my palms the warm fingers
Of numberless friends and I look,
And lo, not a one of them lingers
To give back the pleasure he took;
And I lift my sad eyes to the faces
All tenderly fixed on my own,
But they wither away in grimaces
That scorn me, and leave me alone.

And I turn to the woman that told me
Her love would live on until death
But her arms they no longer enfold me,
Though barely the dew of her breath
Is dry on the forehead so pallid
That droops like the weariest thing
O'er this most inharmonious ballad
That ever a sorrow may sing.

So I'm dazed and bewildered with living
A life but an intricate skein
Of hopes and despairs and thanksgiving
Wound up and unravelled again
Till it seems, whether waking or sleeping,
I am wondering ever the while
At a something that smiles when I'm weeping,
And a something that weeps when I smile.

BRUDDER SIMS

Dah's Brudder Sims! Dast slam yo' Bible shet
An' lef' dat man alone kase he's de boss
Ob all de preachahs ev' I come across!
Day's no twis' in dat gospil book, I bet,
Ut Brudder Sims cain't splanify, an' set
You' min' at eaze! W'at's Moses an' de Laws?
W'at's fo'ty days an' nights ut Noey toss
Aroun' de Dil-ooge? W'at dem Chillen et
De Lo'd rain down? W'at s'prise ole Joney so
In dat whale's inna'ds? W'at dat laddah mean
Ut Jacop see? an' wha' dat laddah go?
Who clim dat laddah? Wha' dat laddah lean?
An' wha' dat laddah now? "Dast chalk yo' toe
Wid Faith," sez Brudder Sims, "an' den you know!"

DEFORMED

Crouched at the corner of the street
She sits all day, with face too white
And hands too wasted to be sweet
In anybody's sight.

Her form is shrunken, and a pair
Of crutches leaning at her side
Are crossed like homely hands in prayer
At quiet eventide.

Her eyes, two lustrous, weary things
Have learned a look that ever aches,
Despite the ready jinglings
The passer's penny makes.

And, noting this, I pause and muse
If any precious promise touch
This heart that has so much to lose
If dreaming overmuch

And, in a vision, mistily
Her future womanhood appears,
A picture framed with agony
And drenched with ceaseless tears

Where never lover comes to claim
The hand outheld so yearningly
The laughing babe that lisps her name
Is but a fantasy!

And, brooding thus, all swift and wild
A daring fancy, strangely sweet,
Comes o'er me, that the crippled child
That crouches at my feet

Has found her head a resting-place
Upon my shoulder, while my kiss
Across the pallor of her face
Leaves crimson trails of bliss.

FAITH

The sea was breaking at my feet,
And looking out across the tide,
Where placid waves and heaven meet,
I thought me of the Other Side.

For on the beach on which I stood

Were wastes of sands, and wash, and roar,
Low clouds, and gloom, and solitude,
And wrecks, and ruins, nothing more.

"O, tell me if beyond the sea
A heavenly port there is!" I cried,
And back the echoes laughingly
"There is! there is!" replied.

THE LOST THRILL

I grow so weary, someway, of all thing
That love and loving have vouchsafed to me,
Since now all dreamed-of sweets of ecstasy
Am I possessed of: The caress that clings
The lips that mix with mine with murmurings
No language may interpret, and the free,
Unfettered brood of kisses, hungrily
Feasting in swarms on honeyed blossomings
Of passion's fullest flower. For yet I miss
The essence that alone makes love divine
The subtle flavoring no tang of this
Weak wine of melody may here define:
A something found and lost in the first kiss
A lover ever poured through lips of mine.

AT DUSK

A something quiet and subdued
In all the faces that we meet;
A sense of rest, a solitude
O'er all the crowded street;
The very noises seem to be
Crude utterings of harmony,
And all we hear, and all we see,
Has in it something sweet.

Thoughts come to us as from a dream
Of some long-vanished yesterday;
The voices of the children seem
Like ours, when young as they;
The hand of Charity extends
To meet Misfortune's, where it blends,
Veiled by the dusk and oh, my friends,
Would it were dusk alway!

ANOTHER RIDE FROM GHENT TO AIX

We sprang for the side-holts, my gripsack and I
It dangled, I dangled, we both dangled by.
"Good speed!" cried mine host, as we landed at last
"Speed?" chuckled the watch we went lumbering past;
Behind shut the switch, and out through the rear door
I glared while we waited a half hour more.

I had missed the express that went thundering down
Ten minutes before to my next lecture town,
And my only hope left was to catch this "wild freight,"
Which the landlord remarked was "most luckily late
But the twenty miles distance was easily done,
If they run half as fast as they usually run!"

Not a word to each other, we struck a snail's pace
Conductor and brakeman ne'er changing a place
Save at the next watering-tank, where they all
Got out, strolled about, cut their names on the wall,
Or listlessly loitered on down to the pile
Of sawed wood just beyond us, to doze for a while.

'Twas high noon at starting, but while we drew near
"Arcady" I said, "We'll not make it, I fear!
I must strike Aix by eight, and it's three o'clock now;
Let me stoke up that engine, and I'll show you how!"
At which the conductor, with patience sublime,
Smiled up from his novel with, "Plenty of time!"

At "Trask," as we jolted stock-still as a stone,
I heard a cow bawl in a five o'clock tone;
And the steam from the saw-mill looked misty and thin,
And the snarl of the saw had been stifled within:
And a frowzy-haired boy, with a hat full of chips,
Came out and stared up with a smile on his lips.

At "Booneville," I groaned, "Can't I telegraph on?"
No! Why? "'Cause the telegraph-man had just gone
To visit his folks in Almo" and one heard
The sharp snap of my teeth through the throat of a word,
That I dragged for a mile and a half up the track,
And strangled it there, and came skulkingly back.

Again we were off. It was twilight, and more,
As we rolled o'er a bridge where beneath us the roar
Of a river came up with so wooing an air
I mechanic'ly strapped myself fast in my chair
As a brakeman slid open the door for more light,
Saying: "Captain, brace up, for your town is in sight!"

"How they'll greet me!" and all in a moment, "chewang!"
And the train stopped again, with a bump and a bang.

What was it? "The section-hands, just in advance."
And I spit on my hands, and I rolled up my pants,
And I clumb like an imp that the fiends had let loose
Up out of the depths of that deadly caboose.

I ran the train's length, I lept safe to the ground
And the legend still lives that for five miles around
They heard my voice hailing the hand-car that yanked
Me aboard at my bidding, and gallantly cranked,
As I grovelled and clung, with my eyes in eclipse,
And a rim of red foam round my rapturous lips.

Then I cast loose my Ulster, each ear-tab let fall
Kicked off both my shoes, let go arctics and all
Stood up with the boys, leaned, patted each head
As it bobbed up and down with the speed that we sped;
Clapped my hands, laughed and sang, any noise, bad or good,
Till at length into Aix we rotated and stood.

And all I remember is friends flocking round
As I unsheathed my head from a hole in the ground;
And no voice but was praising that hand-car divine,
As I rubbed down its spokes with that lecture of mine.
Which (the citizens voted by common consent)
Was no more than its due. 'Twas the lecture they meant.

IN THE HEART OF JUNE
In the heart of June, love,
You and I together,
On from dawn till noon, love,
Laughing with the weather;
Blending both our souls, love,
In the selfsame tune,
Drinking all life holds, love,
In the heart of June.

In the heart of June, love,
With its golden weather,
Underneath the moon, love,
You and I together.
Ah! how sweet to seem, love,
Drugged and half aswoon
With this luscious dream, love,
In the heart of June.

DREAMS
"Do I sleep, do I dream,

Do I wonder and doubt
Are things what they seem
Or is visions about?"

There has always been an inclination, or desire, rather, on my part to believe in the mystic, even as far back as stretches the gum-elastic remembrance of my first "taffy-pullin'" given in honor of my fifth birthday; and the ghost-stories, served by way of ghastly dessert, by our hired girl. In fancy I again live over all the scenes of that eventful night:

The dingy kitchen, with its haunting odors of a thousand feasts and wash-days; the old bench-legged stove, with its happy family of skillets, stewpans and round-bellied kettles crooning and blubbering about it. And how we children clustered round the genial hearth, with the warm smiles dying from our faces just as the embers dimmed and died out in the open grate, as with bated breath we listened to how some one's grandmother had said that her first man went through a graveyard once, one stormy night, "jest to show the neighbors that he wasn't afeard o' nothin'," and how when he was just passing the grave of his first wife "something kind o' big and white-like, with great big eyes like fire, raised up from behind the headboard, and kind o' re'ched out for him"; and how he turned and fled, "with that air white thing after him as tight as it could jump, and a hollerin' 'wough-yough-yough!' till you could hear it furder'n you could a bullgine," and how, at last, just as the brave and daring intruder was clearing two graves and the fence at one despairing leap, the "white thing," had made a grab at him with its iron claws, and had nicked him so close his second wife was occasioned the onerous duty of affixing another patch in his pantaloons. And in conclusion, our hired girl went on to state that this blood-curdling incident had so wrought upon the feelings of "the man that wasn't afeard o' nothin'," and had given him such a distaste for that particular graveyard, that he never visited it again, and even entered a clause in his will to the effect that he would ever remain an unhappy corpse should his remains be interred in said graveyard.

I forgot my pop-corn that night; I forgot my taffy; I forgot all earthly things; and I tossed about so feverishly in my little bed, and withal so restlessly, that more than once my father's admonition above the footboard of the big bed, of "Drat you! go to sleep, there!" foreshadowed my impending doom. And once he leaned over and made a vicious snatch at me, and holding me out at arm's length by one leg, demanded in thunder-tones, "what in the name o' flames and flashes I meant, anyhow!"

I was afraid to stir a muscle from that on, in consequence of which I at length straggled off in fitful dreams and heavens! what dreams! A very long and lank, and slim and slender old woman in white knocked at the door of my vision, and I let her in. She patted me on the head and oh! how cold her hands were! And they were very hard hands, too, and very heavy and, horror of horrors! they were not hands, they were claws! they were iron! they were like the things I had seen the hardware man yank nails out of a keg with. I quailed and shivered till the long and slim and slender old woman jerked my head up and snarled spitefully, "What's the matter with you, bub," and I said, "Nawthin'!" and she said, "Don't you dare to lie to me!" I moaned.

"Don't you like me?" she asked.

I hesitated.

"And lie if you dare!" she said "Don't you like me?"

"Oomh-oomh!" said I.

"Why?" said she.

"Cos, you're too long and slim an'"

"Go on!" said she.

"And tall!" said I.

"Ah, ha!" said she, "and that's it, hey?"

And then she began to grow shorter and thicker, and fatter and squattier.

"And how do I suit you now?" she wheezed at length, when she had wilted down to about the size of a large loaf of bread.

I shook more violently than ever at the fearful spectacle.

"How do you like me now?" she yelped again, "And don't you lie to me neither, or I'll swaller you whole!"

I writhed and hid my face.

"Do you like me?"

"No-o-oh!" I moaned.

She made another snatch at my hair. I felt her jagged claws sink into my very brain. I struggled and she laughed hideously.

"You don't, hey?"

"Yes, yes, I do. I love you!" said I.

"You lie! You lie!" She shrieked derisively. "You know you lie!" and as I felt the iron talons sinking and gritting in my very brain, with one wild, despairing effort, I awoke.

I saw the fire gleaming in the grate, and by the light it made I dimly saw the outline of the old mantelpiece that straddled it, holding the old clock high upon its shoulders. I was awake then, and the little squatty woman with her iron talons was a dream! I felt an oily gladness stealing over me, and yet I shuddered to be all alone.

If only some one were awake, I thought, whose blessed company would drown all recollections of that fearful dream; but I dared not stir or make a noise. I could only hear the ticking of the clock, and my father's sullen snore. I tried to compose my thoughts to pleasant themes, but that telescopic old woman in white would rise up and mock my vain appeals, until in fancy I again saw her altitudinous proportions dwindling into that repulsive and revengeful figure with the iron claws, and I grew restless and attempted to sit up. Heavens! something yet held me by the hair. The chill sweat that betokens speedy dissolution gathered on my brow. I made another effort and arose, that deadly clutch yet fastened in my hair. Could it be possible! The short, white woman still held me in her vengeful grasp! I could see her white dress showing from behind either of my ears. She still clung to me, and with one wild, unearthly cry of "Pap!" I started round the room.

I remember nothing further, until as the glowing morn sifted through the maple at the window, powdering with gold the drear old room, and baptizing with its radiance the anxious group of old home-faces leaning over my bed, I heard my father's voice once more rasping on my senses "Now get the booby up, and wash that infernal wax out of his hair!"

BECAUSE

Why did we meet long years of yore?
And why did we strike hands and say:
"We will be friends, and nothing more";
Why are we musing thus to-day?
Because because was just because,
And no one knew just why it was.

Why did I say good-by to you?
Why did I sail across the main?
Why did I love not heaven's own blue
Until I touched these shores again?
Because because was just because,
And you nor I knew why it was.

Why are my arms about you now,
And happy tears upon your cheek?
And why my kisses on your brow?
Look up in thankfulness and speak!
Because because was just because,
And only God knew why it was.

TO THE CRICKET

The chiming seas may clang; and Tubal Cain
May clink his tinkling metals as he may;
Or Pan may sit and pipe his breath away;
Or Orpheus wake his most entrancing strain
Till not a note of melody remain!
But thou, O cricket, with thy roundelay,
Shalt laugh them all to scorn! So wilt thou, pray,
Trill me thy glad song o'er and o'er again:
I shall not weary; there is purest worth
In thy sweet prattle, since it sings the lone
Heart home again. Thy warbling hath no dearth
Of childish memories no harsher tone
Than we might listen to in gentlest mirth,
Thou poor plebeian minstrel of the hearth.

THE OLD-FASHIONED BIBLE

How dear to my heart are the scenes of my childhood
That now but in mem'ry I sadly review;
The old meeting-house at the edge of the wildwood,
The rail fence and horses all tethered thereto;
The low, sloping roof, and the bell in the steeple,
The doves that came fluttering out overhead
As it solemnly gathered the God-fearing people
To hear the old Bible my grandfather read.
The old-fashioned Bible
The dust-covered Bible
The leathern-bound Bible my grandfather read.

The blessed old volume! The face bent above it
As now I recall it, is gravely severe,
Though the reverent eye that droops downward to love it
Makes grander the text through the lens of a tear,
And, as down his features it trickles and glistens,
The cough of the deacon is stilled, and his head
Like a haloéd patriarch's leans as he listens
To hear the old Bible my grandfather read.
The old-fashioned Bible
The dust-covered Bible
The leathern-bound Bible my grandfather read.

Ah! who shall look backward with scorn and derision
And scoff the old book though it uselessly lies
In the dust of the past, while this newer revision
Lisps on of a hope and a home in the skies?
Shall the voice of the Master be stifled and riven?
Shall we hear but a tithe of the words He has said,
When so long He has, listening, leaned out of Heaven
To hear the old Bible my grandfather read?
The old-fashioned Bible
The dust-covered Bible
The leathern-bound Bible my grandfather read.

UNCOMFORTED

Lelloine! Lelloine! Don't you hear me calling?
Calling through the night for you, and calling through the day;
Calling when the dawn is here, and when the dusk is falling
Calling for my Lelloine the angels lured away!

Lelloine! I call and listen, starting from my pillow
In the hush of midnight, Lelloine! I cry,
And o'er the rainy window-pane I hear the weeping willow
Trail its dripping leaves like baby-fingers in reply.

Lelloine, I miss the glimmer of your glossy tresses,
I miss the dainty velvet palms that nestled in my own;

And all my mother-soul went out in answerless caresses,
And a storm of tears and kisses when you left me here alone.

I have prayed, O Lelloine, but Heaven will not hear me,
I can not gain one sign from Him who leads you by the hand;
And O it seems that ne'er again His mercy will come near me
That He will never see my need, nor ever understand.

Won't you listen, Lelloine? just a little leaning
O'er the walls of Paradise, lean and hear my prayer,
And interpret death to Him in all its awful meaning,
And tell Him you are lonely without your mother there.

WHAT THEY SAID

Whispering to themselves apart,
They who knew her said of her,
"Dying of a broken heart
Death her only comforter
For the man she loved is dead
She will follow soon!" they said.

Beautiful? Ah! brush the dust
From Raphael's fairest face,
And restore it, as it must
First have smiled back from its place
On his easel as he leant
Wrapt in awe and wonderment!

Why, to kiss the very hem
Of the mourning-weeds she wore,
Like the winds that rustled them,
I had gone the round world o'er;
And to touch her hand I swear
All things dareless I would dare!

But unto themselves apart,
Whispering, they said of her,
"Dying of a broken heart
Death her only comforter
For the man she loved is dead
She will follow soon!" they said.

So I mutely turned away,
Turned with sorrow and despair,
Yearning still from day to day
For that woman dying there,
Till at last, by longing led,
I returned to find her dead?

"Dead?" I know that word would tell
Rhyming there but in this case
"Wed" rhymes equally as well
In the very selfsame place
And, in fact, the latter word
Is the one she had preferred.

Yet unto themselves apart,
Whisp'ring they had said of her
"Dying of a broken heart
Death her only comforter
For the man she loved is dead
She will follow soon!" they said.

AFTER THE FROST

After the frost! O the rose is dead,
And the weeds lie pied in the garden-bed,
And the peach tree's shade in the wan sunshine,
Faint as the veins in these hands of mine,
Streaks the gray of the orchard wall
Where the vine rasps loose, and the last leaves fall,
And the bare boughs writhe, and the winds are lost
After the frost, the frost!

After the frost! O the weary head
And the hands and the heart are quietéd;
And the lips we loved are locked at last,
And kiss not back, though the rain falls fast
And the lashes drip, and the soul makes moan,
And on through the dead leaves walks alone
Where the bare boughs writhe and the winds are lost
After the frost, the frost!

CHARLES H. PHILLIPS - OBIT NOVEMBER 5TH, 1881

O friend! There is no way
To bid farewell to thee!
The words that we would say
Above thy grave to-day
Still falter and delay
And fail us utterly.

When walking with us here,
The hand we loved to press
Was gentle, and sincere
As thy frank eyes were clear
Through every smile and tear
Of pleasure and distress.

In years, young; yet in thought
Mature; thy spirit, free,
And fired with fervor caught
Of thy proud sire, who fought
His way to fame, and taught
Its toilsome way to thee.

So even thou hast gained
The victory God-given
Yea, as our cheeks are stained
With tears, and our souls pained
And mute, thou hast attained
Thy high reward in Heaven!

WHEN IT RAINS

When it rains, and with the rain
Never bird has heart to sing,
And across the window-pane
Is no sunlight glimmering;
When the pitiless refrain
Brings a tremor to the lips,
Our tears are like the rain
As it drips, drips, drips
Like the sad, unceasing rain as it drips.

When the light of heaven's blue
Is blurred and blotted quite,
And the dreary day to you
Is but a long twilight;
When it seems that ne'er again
Shall the sun break its eclipse,
Our tears are like the rain
As it drips, drips, drips
Like the endless, friendless rain as it drips.

When it rains! weary heart,
O be of better cheer!
The leaden clouds will part,
And the morrow will be clear;
Take up your load again,
With a prayer upon your lips,
Thanking Heaven for the rain
As it drips, drips, drips
With the golden bow of promise as it drips.

AN ASSASSIN

Cat-like he creeps along where ways are dim,
From covert unto covert's secrecy;
His shadow in the moonlight shrinks from him
And crouches warily.

He hugs strange envies to his breast, and nurses
Wild hatreds, till the murderous hand he grips
Falls, quivering with the tension of the curses
He launches from his lips.

Drenched in his victim's blood he holds high revel;
He mocks at justice, and in all men's eyes
Insults his God and no one but the devil
Is sorry when he dies.

BEST OF ALL

Of all good gifts that the Lord lets fall,
Is not silence the best of all?

The deep, sweet hush when the song is closed,
And every sound but a voiceless ghost;

And every sigh, as we listening leant,
A breathless quiet of vast content?

The laughs we laughed have a purer ring
With but their memory echoing;

And the joys we voiced, and the words we said,
Seem so dearer for being dead.

So of all good gifts that the Lord lets fall,
Is not silence the best of all?

BIN A-FISHIN'

W'en de sun's gone down, un de moon is riz,
Bin a-fishin'! Bin a-fishin'!
It's I's aguine down wha' the by-o is!
Bin a-fishin' all night long!

Chorus

Bin a-fishin'! Bin a-fishin'!
Bin a-fishin' clean fum de dusk of night
Twell away 'long on in de mornin' light.

Bait my hook, un I plunk her down!

Bin a-fishin'! Bin a-fishin'!
Un I lay dat catfish weigh five pound!
Bin a-fishin' all night long!

Chorus

Folks tells me ut a sucker won't bite,
Bin a-fishin'! Bin a-fishin'!
Yit I lif' out fo' last Chuesday night,
Bin a-fishin' all night long!

Chorus

Little fish nibble un de big fish come;
Bin a-fishin'! Bin a-fishin'!
"Go way, little fish! I want some!"
Bin a-fishin' all night long!

Chorus

Sez de bull frog, "D-runk!" sez de ole owl, "Whoo!"
Bin a-fishin'! Bin a-fishin'!
'Spec, Mr. Nigger, dey's a-meanin' you,
Bin a-fishin' all night long!

Chorus

UNCLE DAN'L IN TOWN OVER SUNDAY

I cain't git used to city ways
Ner never could, I' bet my hat!
Jevver know jes' whur I was raised?
Raised on a farm! D' ever tell you that?
Was undoubtatly, I declare!
And now, on Sunday fun to spare
Around a farm! Why jes' to set
Up on the top three-cornered rail
Of Pap's old place, nigh La Fayette,
I'd swap my soul off, hide and tail!
You fellers in the city here,
You don't know nothin'! S'pose to-day,
This clatterin' Sunday, you waked up
Without no jinglin'-janglin' bells,
Ner rattlin' of the milkman's cup,
Ner any swarm of screechin' birds
Like these here English swallers, S'pose
Ut you could miss all noise like those,
And git shet o' thinkin' of 'em afterwerds,
And then, in the country, wake and hear
Nothin' but silence, wake and see

Nothin' but green woods fur and near?
What sort o' Sunday would that be?...
Wisht I hed you home with me!
Now think! The laziest of all days
To git up any time, er sleep
Er jes' lay round and watch the haze
A-dancin' 'crost the wheat, and keep
My pipe a-goern laisurely,
And puff and whiff as pleases me
And ef I leave a trail of smoke
Clean through the house, no one to say,
"Wah! throw that nasty thing away;
Hev some regyard fer decency!"
To walk round barefoot, if you choose;
Er saw the fiddle, er dig some bait
And go a-fishin', er pitch hoss shoes
Out in the shade somewhurs, and wait
For dinner-time, with an appetite
Ut folks in town cain't equal quite!
To laze around the barn and poke
Fer hens' nests, er git up a match
Betwixt the boys, and watch 'em scratch
And rassle round, and sweat and swear
And quarrel to their hearts' content;
And me a-jes' a-settin' there
A-hatchin' out more devilment!
What sort o' Sunday would that be?...
Wisht I hed you home with me!

SOLDIERS HERE TO-DAY

I

Soldiers and saviours of the homes we love;
Heroes and patriots who marched away,
And who marched back, and who marched on above
All, all are here to-day!

By the dear cause you fought for you are here;
At summons of bugle, and the drum
Whose palpitating syllables were ne'er
More musical, you come!

Here by the stars that bloom in fields of blue,
And by the bird above with shielding wings;
And by the flag that floats out over you,
With silken beckonings

Ay, here beneath its folds are gathered all
Who warred unscathed for blessings that it gave
Still blessed its champion, though it but fall

A shadow on his grave!

II

We greet you, Victors, as in vast array
You gather from the scenes of strife and death
From spectral fortress walls where curls away
The cannon's latest breath.

We greet you from the crumbling battlements
Where once again the old flag feels the breeze
Stroke out its tattered stripes and smooth its rents
With rippling ecstasies.

From living tombs where every hope seemed lost
With famine quarantined by bristling guns
The prison pens, the guards, the "dead-line" crossed
By riddled skeletons!

From furrowed plains, sown thick with bursting shells
From mountain gorge, and toppling crags o'erhead
From wards of pestilential hospitals,
And trenches of the dead.

III

In fancy all are here. The night is o'er,
And through dissolving mists the morning gleams;
And clustered round their hearths we see once more
The heroes of our dreams.

Strong, tawny faces, some, and some are fair,
And some are marked with age's latest prime,
And, seer-like, browed and aureoled with hair
As hoar as winter-time.

The faces of fond lovers, glorified
The faces of the husband and the wife
The babe's face nestled at the mother's side,
And smiling back at life;

A bloom of happiness in every cheek
A thrill of tingling joy in every vein
In every soul a rapture they will seek
In Heaven, and find again!

IV

'Tis not a vision only we who pay
But the poor tribute of our praises here
Are equal sharers in the guerdon they
Purchased at price so dear.

The angel, Peace, o'er all uplifts her hand,

Waving the olive, and with heavenly eyes
Shedding a light of love o'er sea and land
As sunshine from the skies

Her figure pedestalled on Freedom's soil
Her sandals kissed with seas of golden grain
Queen of a realm of joy-requited toil
That glories in her reign.

O blessed land of labor and reward!
O gracious Ruler, let Thy reign endure;
In pruning-hook and ploughshare beat the sword,
And reap the harvest sure!

SHADOW AND SHINE

Storms of the winter, and deepening snows,
When will you end? I said,
For the soul within me was numb with woes,
And my heart uncomforted.
When will you cease, O dismal days?
When will you set me free?
For the frozen world and its desolate ways
Are all unloved of me!

I waited long, but the answer came
The kiss of the sunshine lay
Warm as a flame on the lips that frame
The song in my heart to-day.
Blossoms of summer-time waved in the air,
Glimmers of sun in the sea;
Fair thoughts followed me everywhere,
And the world was dear to me.

THAT NIGHT

You and I, and that night, with its perfume and glory!
The scent of the locusts, the light of the moon;
And the violin weaving the waltzers a story,
Enmeshing their feet in the weft of the tune,
Till their shadows uncertain
Reeled round on the curtain,
While under the trellis we drank in the June.

Soaked through with the midnight the cedars were sleeping,
Their shadowy tresses outlined in the bright
Crystal, moon-smitten mists, where the fountain's heart, leaping
Forever, forever burst, full with delight;
And its lisp on my spirit

Fell faint as that near it
Whose love like a lily bloomed out in the night.

O your love was an odorous sachet of blisses!
The breath of your fan was a breeze from Cathay!
And the rose at your throat was a nest of spilled kisses!
And the music! in fancy I hear it to-day,
As I sit here, confessing
Our secret, and blessing
My rival who found us, and waltzed you away.

AUGUST

O mellow month and merry month,
Let me make love to you,
And follow you around the world
As knights their ladies do.
I thought your sisters beautiful,
Both May and April, too,
But April she had rainy eyes,
And May had eyes of blue.

And June I liked the singing
Of her lips and liked her smile
But all her songs were promises
Of something, after while;
And July's face the lights and shades
That may not long beguile
With alterations o'er the wheat
The dreamer at the stile.

But you! ah, you are tropical,
Your beauty is so rare;
Your eyes are clearer, deeper eyes
Than any, anywhere;
Mysterious, imperious,
Deliriously fair,
O listless Andalusian maid,
With bangles in your hair!

THE GUIDE - IMITATED

We rode across the level plain
We my sagacious guide and I.
He knew the earth, the air, the sky;
He knew when it would blow or rain,
And when the weather would be dry:
The blended blades of grass spake out
To him when Redskins were about;

The wagon tracks would tell him too,
The very day that they rolled through:
He knew their burden, whence they came
If any horse along were lame,
And what its owner ought to do;
He knew when it would snow; he knew,
By some strange intuition, when
The buffalo would overflow
The prairies like a flood, and then
Recede in their stampede again.
He knew all things yea, he did know
The brand of liquor in my flask,
And many times did tilt it up,
Nor halt or hesitate one whit,
Nor pause to slip the silver cup
From off its crystal base, nor ask
Why I preferred to drink from it.
And more and more I plied him, and
Did query of him o'er and o'er,
And seek to lure from him the lore
By which the man did understand
These hidden things of sky and land:
And, wrought upon, he sudden drew
His bridle wheeled, and caught my hand
Pressed it, as one that loved me true,
And bade me listen.

There be few
Like tales as strange to listen to!
He told me all. How, when a child,
The Indians stole him, there he laughed
"They stole me, and I stole their craft!"
Then slowly winked both eyes, and smiled,
And went on ramblingly, "And they
They reared me, and I ran away
'Twas winter, and the weather wild;
And, caught up in the awful snows
That bury wilderness and plain,
I struggled on until I froze
My feet ere human hands again
Were reached to me in my distress,
And lo, since then not any rain
May fall upon me anywhere,
Nor any cyclone's cussedness
Slip up behind me unaware,
Nor any change of cold, or heat,
Or blow, or snow, but I do know
It's coming, days and days before;
I know it by my frozen feet
I know it by my itching heels,
And by the agony one feels

Who knows that scratching nevermore
Will bring to him the old and sweet
Relief he knew ere thus endowed
With knowledge that a certain cloud
Will burst with storm on such a day,
And when a snow will fall, and nay,
I speak not falsely when I say
That by my tingling heels and toes
I measure time, and can disclose
The date of month, the week and lo,
The very day and minute, yea
Look at your watch! An hour ago
And twenty minutes I did say
Unto myself with bitter laugh,
'In less than one hour and a half
Will I be drunken!' Is it so?"

SUTTER'S CLAIM - IMITATED

Say! you feller! You
With that spade and the pick!
What do you 'pose to do
On this side o' the crick?
Goin' to tackle this claim? Well, I reckon
You'll let up ag'in, purty quick!

No bluff, understand,
But the same has been tried,
And the claim never panned
Or the fellers has lied,
For they tell of a dozen that tried it,
And quit it most onsatisfied.

The luck's dead ag'in it!
The first man I see
That stuck a pick in it
Proved that thing to me,
For he sort o' took down, and got homesick,
And went back whar he'd orto be!

Then others they worked it
Some more or less,
But finally shirked it,
In grades of distress,
With an eye out, a jaw or skull busted,
Or some sort o' seriousness.

The last one was plucky
He wasn't afeerd,
And bragged he was "lucky,"

And said that "he'd heerd
A heap of bluff-talk," and swore awkard
He'd work any claim that he keered!

Don't you strike nary lick
With that pick till I'm through;
This-here feller talked slick
And as peart-like as you!
And he says: "I'll abide here
As long as I please!"
But he didn't.... He died here
And I'm his disease!

HER LIGHT GUITAR

She twankled a tune on her light guitar
A low, sweet jangle of tangled sounds,
As blurred as the voices of the fairies are,
Dancing in moondawn dales and downs;
And the tinkling drip of the strange refrain
Ran over the rim of my soul like rain.

The great blond moon in the midnight skies
Paused and poised o'er the trellis eaves,
And the stars, in the light of her upturned eyes,
Sifted their love through the rifted leaves,
Glittered and splintered in crystal mist
Down the glittering strings that her fingers kissed.

O the melody mad! O the tinkle and thrill
Of the ecstasy of the exquisite thing!
The red rose dropped from the window-sill
And lay in a long swoon quivering;
While the dying notes of the strain divine
Rippled in glee up my spellbound spine.

WHILE CIGARETTES TO ASHES TURN

I

"He smokes and that's enough," says Ma
"And cigarettes, at that!" says Pa.

"He must not call again," says she
"He shall not call again!" says he.

They both glare at me as before
Then quit the room and bang the door.

While I, their wilful daughter, say,

"I guess I'll love him, anyway!"

II

At twilight, in his room, alone,
His careless feet inertly thrown

Across a chair, my fancy can
But worship this most worthless man!

I dream what joy it is to set
His slow lips round a cigarette,

With idle-humored whiff and puff
Ah! this is innocent enough!

To mark the slender fingers raise
The waxen match's dainty blaze,

Whose chastened light an instant glows
On drooping lids and arching nose,

Then, in the sudden gloom, instead,
A tiny ember, dim and red,

Blooms languidly to ripeness, then
Fades slowly, and grows ripe again.

III

I lean back, in my own boudoir
The door is fast, the sash ajar;

And in the dark, I smiling stare
At one wide window over there,

Where some one, smoking, pinks the gloom,
The darling darkness of his room!

I push my shutters wider yet,
And lo! I light a cigarette;

And gleam for gleam, and glow for glow,
Each pulse of light a word we know,

We talk of love that still will burn
While cigarettes to ashes turn.

TWO SONNETS TO THE JUNE-BUG
I
You make me jes' a little nervouser

Than any dog-gone bug I ever see!
And you know night's the time to pester me
When any tetch at all 'll rub the fur
Of all my patience back'ards! You're the myrrh
And ruburb of my life! A bumblebee
Cain't hold a candle to you; and a he
Bald hornet, with a laminated spur
In his hip pocket, daresent even cheep
When you're around! And, dern ye! you have made
Me lose whole ricks and stacks and piles of sleep,
And many of a livelong night I've laid
And never shut an eye, hearin' you keep
Up that eternal buzzin' serenade!

II

And I've got up and lit the lamp, and clum
On cheers and trunks and wash-stands and bureaus,
And all such dangerous articles as those,
And biffed at you with brooms, and never come
'In two feet of you, maybe skeered you some,
But what does that amount to when it throws
A feller out o' balance, and his nose
Gits barked ag'inst the mantel, while you hum
Fer joy around the room, and churn your head
Ag'inst the ceilin', and draw back and butt
The plasterin' loose, and drop behind the bed,
Where never human-bein' ever putt
Harm's hand on you, er ever truthful said
He'd choked yer dern infernal wizzen shut!

AUTOGRAPHIC - For an Album
I feel, if aught I ought to rhyme,
I ought 'a' thought a longer time,
And ought 'a' caught a higher sense,
Of autocratic eloquence.
I ought 'a' sought each haughty Muse
That taught a thought I ought to use,
And fought and fraught, and so devised
A poem unmonotonized.
But since all this was vain, I thought
I ought to simply say, I ought
To thank you, as I ought to do,
And ought to bow my best to you;
And ought to trust not to intrude
A rudely wrought-up gratitude,
But ought to smile, and ought to laugh,
And ought to write an autograph.

AN IMPROMPTU ON ROLLER SKATES

Rumble, tumble, growl, and grate!
Skip, and trip, and gravitate!
Lunge, and plunge, and thrash the planks
With your blameless, shameless shanks:
In excruciating pain,
Stand upon your head again,
And, uncoiling kink by kink,
Kick the roof out of the rink!

In derisive bursts of mirth,
Drop ka-whop and jar the earth!
Jolt your lungs down in your socks,
Oh! tempestuous equinox
Of dismembered legs and arms!
Strew your ways with wild alarms;
Fameward skoot and ricochet
On your glittering vertebræ!

WRITTEN IN BUNNER'S "AIRS FROM ARCADY"

O ever gracious Airs from Arcady!
What lack is there of any jocund thing
In glancing wit or glad imagining
Capricious fancy may not find in thee?
The laugh of Momus, tempered daintily
To lull the ear and lure its listening;
The whistled syllables the birds of spring
Flaunt ever at our guessings what they be;
The wood, the seashore, and the clanging town;
The pets of fashion, and the ways of such;
The robe de chambre, and the russet gown;
The lordling's carriage, and the pilgrim's crutch
From hale old Chaucer's wholesomeness, clean down
To our artistic Dobson's deftest touch!

IN THE AFTERNOON

You in the hammock; and I, near by,
Was trying to read, and to swing you, too;
And the green of the sward was so kind to the eye,
And the shade of the maples so cool and blue,
That often I looked from the book to you
To say as much, with a sigh.

You in the hammock. The book we'd brought
From the parlor to read in the open air,
Something of love and of Launcelot

And Guinevere, I believe, was there
But the afternoon, it was far more fair
Than the poem was, I thought.

You in the hammock; and on and on
I droned and droned through the rhythmic stuff
But, with always a half of my vision gone
Over the top of the page, enough
To caressingly gaze at you, swathed in the fluff
Of your hair and your odorous "lawn."

You in the hammock and that was a year
Fully a year ago, I guess
And what do we care for their Guinevere
And her Launcelot and their lordliness!
You in the hammock still, and Yes
Kiss me again, my dear!

AT MADAME MANICURE'S

Daintiest of Manicures!
What a cunning hand is yours;
And how awkward, rude and great
Mine, as you manipulate!
Wonderfully cool and calm
Are the touches of your palm
To my fingers, as they rest
In their rosy, cosey nest,
While your own, with deftest skill,
Dance and caper as they will,
Armed with instruments that seem
Gathered from some fairy dream
Tiny spears, and simitars
Such as pixy armorers
Might have made for jocund fays
To parade on holidays,
And flash round in dewy dells,
Lopping down the lily-bells;
Or in tilting, o'er the leas,
At the clumsy bumblebees,
Splintering their stings, perchance,
As the knights in old romance
Snapped the spears of foes that fought
In the jousts at Camelot!
Smiling? Dainty Manicure?
'Twould delight me, but that you're
Simply smiling, as I see,
At my nails and not at me!
Haply this is why they glow
And light up and twinkle so!

A CALLER FROM BOONE - BENJ. F. JOHNSON VISITS THE EDITOR

It was a dim and chill and loveless afternoon in the late fall of eighty-three when I first saw the genial subject of this hasty sketch. From time to time the daily paper on which I worked had been receiving, among the general literary driftage of amateur essayists, poets and sketch-writers, some conceits in verse that struck the editorial head as decidedly novel; and, as they were evidently the production of an unlettered man, and an old man, and a farmer at that, they were usually spared the waste-basket, and preserved, not for publication, but to pass from hand to hand among the members of the staff as simply quaint and mirth-provoking specimens of the verdancy of both the venerable author and the Muse inspiring him. Letters as quaint as were the poems invariably accompanied them, and the oddity of these, in fact, had first called attention to the verses. I well remember the general merriment of the office when the first of the old man's letters was read aloud, and I recall, too, some of his comments on his own verse, verbatim. In one place he said: "I make no doubt you will find some purty sad spots in my poetry, considerin'; but I hope you will bear in mind that I am a great sufferer with rheumatizum, and have been, off and on, sence the cold New Year's. In the main, however," he continued, "I allus aim to write in a cheerful, comfortin' sperit, so's ef the stuff hangs fire, and don't do no good, it hain't a-goin' to do no harm, and them's my honest views on poetry."

In another letter, evidently suspecting his poem had not appeared in print because of its dejected tone, he said: "The poetry I herewith send was wrote off on the finest Autumn day I ever laid eyes on! I never felt better in my life. The morning air was as invigoratin' as bitters with tanzy in it, and the folks at breakfast said they never saw such a' appetite on mortal man before. Then I lit out for the barn, and after feedin', I come back and tuck my pen and ink out on the porch, and jest cut loose. I writ and writ till my fingers was that cramped I couldn't hardly let go of the penholder. And the poem I send you is the upshot of it all. Ef you don't find it cheerful enough fer your columns, I'll have to knock under, that's all!" And that poem, as I recall it, certainly was cheerful enough for publication, only the "copy" was almost undecipherable, and the ink, too, so pale and vague, it was thought best to reserve the verses, for the time, at least, and later on revise, copy, punctuate, and then print it sometime, as much for the joke of it as anything. But it was still delayed, neglected, and in a week's time almost entirely forgotten. And so it was, upon this chill and sombre afternoon I speak of that an event occurred which most pleasantly reminded me of both the poem with the "sad spots" in it, and the "cheerful" one, "writ out on the porch" that glorious autumn day that poured its glory through the old man's letter to us.

Outside and in the sanctum the gloom was too oppressive to permit an elevated tendency of either thought or spirit. I could do nothing but sit listless and inert. Paper and pencil were before me, but I could not write, I could not even think coherently, and was on the point of rising and rushing out into the streets for a wild walk, when there came a hesitating knock at the door.

"Come in!" I snarled, grabbing up my pencil and assuming a frightfully industrious air: "Come in!" I almost savagely repeated, "Come in! And shut the door behind you!" and I dropped my lids, bent my gaze fixedly upon the blank pages before me and began scrawling some disconnected nothings with no head or tail or anything.

"Sir; howdy," said a low and pleasant voice. And at once, in spite of my perverse resolve, I looked up. I someway felt rebuked.

The speaker was very slowly, noiselessly closing the door. I could hardly face him when he turned around. An old man, of sixty-five, at least, but with a face and an eye of the most cheery and wholesome expression I had ever seen in either youth or age. Over his broad bronzed forehead and white hair he wore a low-crowned, wide-brimmed black felt hat, somewhat rusted now, and with the band grease-crusted, and the binding frayed at intervals, and sagging from the threads that held it on. An old-styled frock coat of black, dull brown in streaks, and quite shiny about the collar and lapels. A waistcoat of no describable material or pattern, and a clean white shirt and collar of one piece, with a black string-tie and double bow, which would have been entirely concealed beneath the long white beard but for its having worked around to one side of the neck. The front outline of the face was cleanly shaven, and the beard, growing simply from the under chin and throat, lent the old pioneer the rather singular appearance of having hair all over him with this luxurious growth pulled out above his collar for mere sample.

I arose and asked the old man to sit down, handing him a chair decorously.

"No, no," he said, "I'm much obleeged. I hain't come in to bother you no more'n I can he'p. All I wanted was to know ef you got my poetry all right. You know I take yer paper," he went on, in an explanatory way, "and seein' you printed poetry in it once-in-a-while, I sent you some of mine, neighbors kindo' advised me to," he added apologetically, "and so I sent you some, two or three times I sent you some, but I hain't never seed hide-ner-hair of it in your paper, and as I wus in town to-day, anyhow, I jest thought I'd kindo' drap in and git it back, ef you ain't goin' to print it, 'cause I allus save up most the things I write, aimin' sometime to git 'em all struck off in pamphlet-form, to kindo' distribit round 'mongst the neighbors, don't you know."

Already I had begun to suspect my visitor's identity, and was mechanically opening the drawer of our poetical department.

"How was your poetry signed?" I asked.

"Signed by my own name," he answered proudly, "signed by my own name, Johnson, Benjamin F. Johnson, of Boone County, this state."

"And is this one of them, Mr. Johnson?" I asked, unfolding a clumsily-folded manuscript, and closely scrutinizing the verse.

"How does she read?" said the old man eagerly, and searching in the meantime for his spectacles. "How does she read? Then I can tell you!"

"It reads," said I, studiously conning the old man's bold but bad chirography, and tilting my chair back indolently, "it reads like this, the first verse does," and I very gravely read:

"Oh! the old swimmin'-hole!"

"Stop! Stop!" said the old man excitedly, "Stop right there! That's my poetry, but that's not the way to read it by a long shot! Give it to me!" and he almost snatched it from my hand. "Poetry like this ain't no poetry at all, 'less you read it natchurl and in jes the same sperit 'at it's writ in, don't you understand. It's a' old man a-talkin', rickollect, and a-feelin' kindo' sad, and yit kindo' sorto' good, too, and I opine he wouldn't got that off with a face on him like a' undertaker, and a voice as solemn as a cow-bell after dark! He'd say it more like this." And the old man adjusted his spectacles and read:

"THE OLD SWIMMIN'-HOLE"
"Oh! the old swimmin'-hole! whare the crick so still and deep
Looked like a baby-river that was laying half asleep,
And the gurgle of the worter round the drift jest below
Sounded like the laugh of something we onc't ust to know
Before we could remember anything but the eyes
Of the angels lookin' out as we left Paradise;
But the merry days of youth is beyond our controle,
And it's hard to part ferever with the old swimmin'-hole."

I clapped my hands in genuine applause. "Read on!" I said, "Read on! Read all of it!"

The old man's face was radiant as he continued:

"Oh! the old swimmin'-hole! In the happy days of yore,
When I ust to lean above it on the old sickamore,
Oh! it showed me a face in its warm sunny tide
That gazed back at me so gay and glorified,
It made me love myself, as I leaped to caress
My shadder smilin' up at me with sich tenderness.
But them days is past and gone, and old Time's tuck his toll
From the old man come back to the old swimmin'-hole.

"Oh! the old swimmin'-hole! In the long, lazy days
When the hum-drum of school made so many run-a-ways,
How pleasant was the jurney down the old dusty lane,
Whare the tracks of our bare feet was all printed so plane
You could tell by the dent of the heel and the sole
They was lots o' fun on hands at the old swimmin'-hole.
But the lost joys is past! Let your tears in sorrow roll
Like the rain that ust to dapple up the old swimmin'-hole.

"Thare the bullrushes growed, and the cattails so tall,
And the sunshine and shadder fell over it all;
And it mottled the worter with amber and gold
Tel the glad lillies rocked in the ripples that rolled;
And the snake-feeder's four gauzy wings fluttered by
Like the ghost of a daisy dropped out of the sky,
Or a wownded apple-blossom in the breeze's controle
As it cut acrost some orchurd to'rds the old swimmin'-hole.

"Oh! the old swimmin'-hole! When I last saw the place,
The scenes was all changed, like the change in my face;
The bridge of the railroad now crosses the spot
Whare the old divin'-log lays sunk and fergot.
And I strayed down the banks whare the trees ust to be
But never again will theyr shade shelter me!
And I wisht in my sorrow I could strip to the soul,
And dive off in my grave like the old swimmin'-hole."

My applause was long and loud. The old man's interpretation of the poem was a positive revelation, though I was glad enough to conceal from him my moistened eyes by looking through the scraps for other specimens of his verse.

"Here," said I enthusiastically, "is another one, signed 'Benj. F. Johnson,' read me this," and I handed him the poem.

The old man smiled and took the manuscript. "This-here one's on 'The Hoss,'" he said, simply clearing his throat. "They ain't so much fancy-work about this as the other'n, but they's jest as much fact, you can bet 'cause, they're no animal a-livin' 'at I love better 'an

"THE HOSS"
"The hoss he is a splendud beast;
He is man's friend, as heaven desined,
And, search the world from west to east,
No honester you'll ever find!

"Some calls the hoss 'a pore dumb brute,'
And yit, like Him who died fer you,
I say, as I theyr charge refute,
'Fergive; they know not what they do!'

"No wiser animal makes tracks
Upon these earthly shores, and hence
Arose the axium, true as facts,
Extoled by all, as 'Good hoss-sense!'

"The hoss is strong, and knows his stren'th,
You hitch him up a time er two
And lash him, and he'll go his len'th
And kick the dashboard out fer you!

"But, treat him allus good and kind,
And never strike him with a stick,
Ner aggervate him, and you'll find
He'll never do a hostile trick.

"A hoss whose master tends him right
And worters him with daily care,
Will do your biddin' with delight,
And act as docile as you air.

"He'll paw and prance to hear your praise,
Because he's learnt to love you well;
And, though you can't tell what he says,
He'll nicker all he wants to tell.

"He knows you when you slam the gate
At early dawn, upon your way
Unto the barn, and snorts elate,
To git his corn, er oats, er hay.

"He knows you, as the orphant knows
The folks that loves her like theyr own,
And raises her and 'finds' her clothes,
And 'schools' her tel a womern-grown!

"I claim no hoss will harm a man,
Ner kick, ner run away, cavort,
Stump-suck, er balk, er 'catamaran,'
Ef you'll jest treat him as you ort.

"But when I see the beast abused
And clubbed around as I've saw some,
I want to see his owner noosed,
And jest yanked up like Absolum!

"Of course they's differunce in stock,
A hoss that has a little yeer,
And slender build, and shaller hock,
Can beat his shadder, mighty near!

"Whilse one that's thick in neck and chist
And big in leg and full in flank,
That tries to race, I still insist
He'll have to take the second rank.

"And I have jest laid back and laughed,
And rolled and wallered in the grass
At fairs, to see some heavy-draft
Lead out at first, yit come in last!

"Each hoss has his appinted place,
The heavy hoss should plow the soil;
The blooded racer, he must race,
And win big wages fer his toil.

"I never bet ner never wrought
Upon my feller-man to bet
And yit, at times, I've often thought
Of my convictions with regret.

"I bless the hoss from hoof to head
From head to hoof, and tale to mane!
I bless the hoss, as I have said,
From head to hoof, and back again!

"I love my God the first of all,
Then Him that perished on the cross,
And next, my wife, and then I fall
Down on my knees and love the hoss."

Again I applauded, handing the old man still another of his poems, and the last received. "Ah!" said he, as his gentle eyes bent on the title; "this-here's the cheerfullest one of 'em all. This is the one writ, as I wrote you about on that glorious October morning two weeks ago I thought your paper would print this-un, shore!"

"Oh, it will print it," I said eagerly; "and it will print the other two as well! It will print anything that you may do us the honor to offer, and we'll reward you beside just as you may see fit to designate. But go on, go on! Read me the poem."

The old man's eyes were glistening as he responded with the poem entitled

"WHEN THE FROST IS ON THE PUNKIN"
"When the frost is on the punkin and the fodder's in the shock,
And you hear the kyouck and gobble of the struttin' turkey-cock,
And the clackin' of the guineys, and the cluckin' of the hens,
And the rooster's hallylooyer as he tiptoes on the fence;
O, it's then's the times a feller is a-feelin' at his best,
With the risin' sun to greet him from a night of peaceful rest,
As he leaves the house, bareheaded, and goes out to feed the stock,
When the frost is on the punkin and the fodder's in the shock.

"They's something kindo' harty-like about the atmusfere
When the heat of summer's over and the coolin' fall is here
Of course we miss the flowers, and the blossums on the trees,
And the mumble of the hummin'-birds and buzzin' of the bees;
But the air's so appetizin'; and the landscape through the haze
Of a crisp and sunny morning of the airly autumn days
Is a pictur' that no painter has the colorin' to mock
When the frost is on the punkin and the fodder's in the shock.

"The husky, rusty russel of the tossels of the corn,
And the raspin' of the tangled leaves, as golden as the morn;
The stubble in the furries, kindo' lonesome-like, but still
A-preachin' sermuns to us of the barns they growed to fill;
The strawstack in the medder, and the reaper in the shed;
The hosses in theyr stalls below, the clover overhead!
O, it sets my hart a-clickin' like the tickin' of a clock,
When the frost is on the punkin and the fodder's in the shock!

"Then your apples all is getherd, and the ones a feller keeps
Is poured around the celler-floor in red and yeller heaps;
And your cider-makin' 's over, and your wimmern-folks is through
With theyr mince and apple-butter, and theyr souse and saussage, too!...
I don't know how to tell it but ef sich a thing could be
As the Angels wantin' boardin', and they'd call around on me
I'd want to 'commodate 'em, all the whole-indurin' flock
When the frost is on the punkin and the fodder's in the shock!"

That was enough! "Surely," thought I, "here is a diamond in the rough, and a 'gem,' too, 'of purest ray serene'!" I caught the old man's hand and wrung it with positive rapture; and it is needless to go further in explanation of how the readers of our daily came to an acquaintance through its columns with the crude, unpolished, yet most gentle genius of Benj. F. Johnson, of Boone.

LORD BACON - WRITTEN AS A JOKE AND ASCRIBED TO A VERY PRACTICAL BUSINESS MAN, AMOS J. WALKER

Master of masters in the days of yore,
When art met insult, with no law's redress;
When Law itself insulted Righteousness,
And Ignorance thine own scholastic lore,
And thou thine own judicial office more,
What master living now canst love thee less,
Seeing thou didst thy greatest art repress
And leave the years its riches to restore
To us, thy long neglectors. Yield us grace
To make becoming recompense, and dawn
On us thy poet-smile; nor let us trace,
In fancy, where the old-world myths have gone,
The shade of Shakespeare, with averted face,
Withdrawn to uttermost oblivion.

MY FIRST WOMERN

I buried my first womern
In the spring; and in the fall
I was married to my second,
And hain't settled yit at all!
Fer I'm allus thinkin', thinkin'
Of the first one's peaceful ways,
A-bilin' soap and singin'
Of the Lord's amazin' grace.

And I'm thinkin' of her, constant,
Dyin' carpet chain and stuff,
And a-makin' up rag carpets,
When the floor was good enough!
And I mind her he'p a-feedin',
And I riccollect her now
A-drappin' corn, and keepin'
Clos't behind me and the plow!

And I'm allus thinkin' of her
Reddin' up around the house;
Er cookin' fer the farm-hands;
Er a-drivin' up the cows.
And there she lays out yander
By the lower medder fence,
Where the cows was barely grazin',
And they're usin' ever sence.

And when I look acrost there
Say it's when the clover's ripe,
And I'm settin', in the evenin',
On the porch here, with my pipe,
And the other'n hollers "Henry!"
W'y they ain't no sadder thing
Than to think of my first womern
And her funeral last spring
Was a year ago

AS WE READ BURNS

Who is speaking? Who has spoken?
Whose voice ceasing thus has broken
The sweet pathos of our dreams?
Sweetest bard of sweetest themes,
Pouring in each poet-heart
Some rare essence of your art
Till it seems your singing lip
Kisses every pencil tip!
Far across the unknown lands
Reach of heavenly isle and sea
How we long to touch the hands
You outhold so lovingly!

TO JAMES NEWTON MATTHEWS - IN ANSWER TO A LETTER ON THE ANATOMY OF THE SONNET

Oho! ye sunny, sonnet-singin' vagrant,
Flauntin' your simmer sangs in sic a weather!
Ane maist can straik the bluebells and the heather
Keekin' aboon the snaw and bloomin' fragrant!
Whiles you, ye whustlin' brither, sic a lay grant
O' a' these janglin', wranglin' sweets thegither,
I weel maun perk my ain doon-drappin' feather
And pipe a wee: Tho' boisterous and flagrant
The winds blow whuzzle-whazzle rhymes that trickle
Fra' aff my tongue less limpid than I'd ha'e them,
I in their little music hap a mickle
O' canty praises, a' asklent to weigh them
Agen your pride, and smile to see them tickle
The warm nest o' the heart wherein I lay them.

SONG

O I would I had a lover!
A lover! a lover!
O I would I had a lover

With a twinkering guitar,
To come beneath my casement
Singing "There is none above her,"
While I, leaning, seemed to hover
In the scent of his cigar!

Then at morn I'd want to meet him
To meet him! to meet him!
O at morn I'd want to meet him,
When the mist was in the sky,
And the dew along the path I went
To casually greet him,
And to cavalierly treat him,
And regret it by and by.

And I'd want to meet his brother
His brother! his brother!
O I'd want to meet his brother
At the german or the play,
To pin a rose on his lapel
And lightly press the other,
And love him like a mother
While he thought the other way.

O I'd pitilessly test him!
And test him! and test him!
O I'd pitilessly test him
Far beyond his own control;
And every tantalizing lure
With which I could arrest him,
I'd loosen to molest him,
Till I tried his very soul.

But ah, when I relented
Relented, relented!
But ah, when I relented
When the stars were blurred and dim,
And the moon above, with crescent grace,
Looked off as I repented,
And with rapture half demented,
All my heart went out to him!

WHEN WE THREE MEET

When we three meet? Ah! friend of mine
Whose verses well and flow as wine,
My thirsting fancy thou dost fill
With draughts delicious, sweeter still
Since tasted by those lips of thine.

I pledge thee, through the chill sunshine
Of autumn, with a warmth divine,
Thrilled through as only I shall thrill
When we three meet.

I pledge thee, if we fast or dine,
We yet shall loosen, line by line,
Old ballads, and the blither trill
Of our-time singers, for there will
Be with us all the Muses nine
When we three meet.

JOSH BILLINGS - DEAD IN CALIFORNIA, OCTOBER 15, 1885

Jolly-hearted old Josh Billings,
With his wisdom and his wit,
And his gravity of presence,
And the drollery of it!
Has he left us, and forever?
When so many merry years
He has only left us laughing
And he leaves us now in tears?

Has he turned from his "Deer Publik,"
With his slyly twinkling eyes
Now grown dim and heavy-lidded
In despite of sunny skies?
Yet with rugged brow uplifted,
And the long hair tossed away,
Like an old heroic lion,
With a mane of iron-gray.

Though we lose him, still we find him
In the mirth of every lip,
And we fare through all his pages
In his glad companionship:
His voice is wed with Nature's,
Laughing in each woody nook
With the chirrup of the robin
And the chuckle of the brook.

But the children, O the children!
They who leaped to his caress,
And felt his arms about them,
And his love and tenderness,
Where, where will they find comfort
As their tears fall like the rain,
And they swarm his face with kisses
That he answers not again?

WHICH ANE

Which ane, an' which ane,
An' which ane for thee?
Here thou hast thy vera choice,
An' which sall it be?
Ye hae the Holy Brither,
An' ye hae the Scholarly;
An', last, ye hae the butt o' baith
Which sall it be?

Ane's oot o' Edinborough,
Wi' the Beuk an' Gown;
An' ane's cam frae Cambridge;
An' ane frae scaur an' down:
An' Deil tak the hindmaist!
Sae the test gaes roun':
An' here ye hae the lairdly twa,
An' ane frae scaur an' down.

Yon's Melancholy
An' the pipes a-skirlin'
Gangs limp an' droopet,
Like a coof at hirlin',
Droopet aye his lang skirts
I' the wins unfurlin';
Yon's Melancholy
An' the pipes a-skirlin'!

Which ane, an' which ane,
An' which ane for thee?
Here thou hast thy vera choice,
An' which sall it be?
Ye hae the Holy Brither,
An' ye hae the Scholarly;
An', last, ye hae the butt o' baith
Which sall it be?

Elbuck ye'r bag, mon!
An' pipe as ye'd burst!
Can ye gie's a waur, mon
E'en than the first?
Be it Meister Wisemon,
I' the classics versed,
An' a slawer gait yet
E'en than the first?

Then gie us Merriment:
Loose him like a linnet
Teeterin' on a bloomin' spray

We ken him i' the minute,
Twinklin' is ane ee asklent,
Wi' auld Clootie in it
Auld Sawney Lintwhite,
We ken him i' the minute!

An' which ane, an' which ane,
An' which ane for thee?
For thou shalt hae thy vera choice,
An' which sall it be?
Ye hae the Holy Brither,
An' ye hae the Scholarly;
A' last, ye hae the butt o' baith
Which sall it be?

THE EARTHQUAKE - CHARLESTON, SEPTEMBER 1, 1886

An hour ago the lulling twilight leant
Above us like a gentle nurse who slips
A slow palm o'er our eyes, in soft eclipse
Of feigned slumber of most sweet content.
The fragrant zephyrs of the tropic went
And came across the senses, like to sips
Of lovers' kisses, when upon her lips
Silence sets finger in grave merriment.
Then sudden did the earth moan as it slept,
And start as one in evil dreams, and toss
Its peopled arms up, as the horror crept,
And with vast breast upheaved and rent across,
Fling down the storied citadel where wept,
And still shall weep, a world above its loss.

A FALL-CRICK VIEW OF THE EARTHQUAKE

I kin hump my back and take the rain,
And I don't keer how she pours;
I kin keep kind o' ca'm in a thunder-storm,
No matter how loud she roars;
I hain't much skeered o' the lightnin',
Ner I hain't sich awful shakes
Afeard o' cyclones but I don't want none
O' yer dad-burned old earthquakes!

As long as my legs keeps stiddy,
And long as my head keeps plum',
And the buildin' stays in the front lot,
I still kin whistle, some!
But about the time the old clock
Flops off'n the mantel-shelf,

And the bureau skoots fer the kitchen,
I'm a-goin' to skoot, myself!

Plague-take! ef you keep me stabled
While any earthquakes is around!
I'm jes' like the stock, I'll beller
And break fer the open ground!
And I 'low you'd be as nervous
And in jes' about my fix,
When yer whole farm slides from in-under you,
And on'y the mor'gage sticks!

Now cars hain't a-goin' to kill you
Ef you don't drive 'crost the track;
Crediters never'll jerk you up
Ef you go and pay 'em back;
You kin stand all moral and mundane storms
Ef you'll on'y jes' behave
But a' EARTHQUAKE: Well, ef it wanted you
It 'ud husk you out o' yer grave!

In the midmost glee of the Christmas
And the mirth of the glad New Year,
A guest has turned from the revel,
And we sit in silence here.

The band chimes on, yet we listen
Not to the air's refrain,
But over it ever we strive to catch
The sound of his voice again;

For the sound of his voice was music,
Dearer than any note
Shook from the strands of harp-strings,
Or poured from the bugle's throat.

A voice of such various ranges,
His utterance rang from the height
Of every rapture, down to the sobs
Of every lost delight.

Though he knew Man's force and his purpose,
As strong as his strongest peers,
He knew, as well, the kindly heart,
And the tenderness of tears.

So is it the face we remember
Shall be always as a child's

That, grieved some way to the very soul,
Looks bravely up and smiles.

O brave it shall look, as it looked its last
On the little daughter's face
Pictured only against the wall,
In its old accustomed place

Where the last gleam of the lamplight
Out of the midnight dim
Yielded its grace, and the earliest dawn
Gave it again to him.

IN DAYS TO COME

In days to come whatever ache
Of age shall rack our bones, or quake
Our slackened thews whatever grip
Rheumatic catch us i' the hip,
We, each one, for the other's sake,
Will of our very wailings make
Such quips of song as well may shake
The spasm'd corners from the lip
In days to come.

Ho! ho! how our old hearts shall rake
The past up! how our dry eyes slake
Their sight upon the dewy drip
Of juicy-ripe companionship,
And blink stars from the blind opaque
In days to come.

LUTHER A. TODD - OBIT JULY 27, 1887, KANSAS CITY, MISSOURI

Gifted, and loved, and praised
By every friend;
Never a murmur raised
Against him, to the end!
With tireless interest
He wrought as he thought best,
And lo, we bend
Where now he takes his rest!

His heart was loyal, to
Its latest thrill,
To the home-loves he knew
And now forever will,
Mother and brother they
The first to pass away,

And, lingering still,
The sister bowed to-day.

Pure as a rose might be,
And sweet, and white,
His father's memory
Was with him day and night:
He spoke of him, as one
May now speak of the son,
Sadly and tenderly,
Yet as a trump had done.

Say, then, of him: He knew
Full depths of care
And stress of pain, and you
Do him scant justice there,
Yet in the lifted face
Grief left not any trace,
Nor mark unfair,
To mar its manly grace.

It was as if each day
Some new hope dawned
Each blessing in delay,
To him, was just beyond;
Between whiles, waiting, he
Drew pictures, cunningly
Fantastic fond
Things that we laughed to see.

Sometimes, as we looked on
His crayon's work,
Some angel-face would dawn
Out radiant, from the mirk
Of features old and thin,
Or jowled with double-chin,
And eyes asmirk,
And gaping mouths agrin.

That humor in his art,
Of genius born,
Welled warmly from a heart
That could not but adorn
All things it touched with love
The eagle, as the dove
The burst of morn
The night the stars above.

Sometimes, amid the wild
Of faces queer,
A mother, with her child

Pressed warm and close to her;
This, I have thought, somehow,
The wife, with head abow,
Unreconciled,
In the great shadow now.

O you of sobbing breath,
Put by all sighs
Of anguish at his death
Turn as he turned his eyes,
In that last hour, unknown
In strange lands, all alone
Turn thine eyes toward the skies,
And, smiling, cease thy moan.

WHEN THE HEARSE COMES BACK

A thing 'at's 'bout as tryin' as a healthy man kin meet
Is some poor feller's funeral a-joggin' 'long the street:
The slow hearse and the hosses, slow enough, to say the least,
Fer to even tax the patience of the gentleman deceased!
The low scrunch of the gravel and the slow grind of the wheels,
The low, slow go of ev'ry woe 'at ev'rybody feels!
So I ruther like the contrast when I hear the whiplash crack
A quickstep fer the hosses,
When the
Hearse
Comes
Back!

Meet it goin' to'rds the cimet'ry, you'll want to drap yer eyes
But ef the plumes don't fetch you, it'll ketch you otherwise
You'll haf to see the caskit, though you'd ort to look away
And 'conomize and save yer sighs fer any other day!
Yer sympathizin' won't wake up the sleeper from his rest
Yer tears won't thaw them hands o' his 'at's froze acrost his breast!
And this is why when airth and sky's a-gittin' blurred and black
I like the flash and hurry
When the
Hearse
Comes
Back!

It's not 'cause I don't 'preciate it ain't no time fer jokes,
Ner 'cause I' got no common human feelin' fer the folks;
I've went to funerals myse'f, and tuk on some, perhaps
Fer my heart's 'bout as mal'able as any other chap's,
I've buried father, mother but I'll haf to jes' git you
To "excuse me," as the feller says. The p'int I'm drivin' to
Is, simply, when we're plum broke down and all knocked out o' whack,

It he'ps to shape us up, like,
When the
Hearse
Comes
Back!

The idy! wadin' round here over shoe-mouth deep in woe,
When they's a graded 'pike o' joy and sunshine, don't you know!
When evening strikes the pastur', cows'll pull out fer the bars
And skittish-like from out the night'll prance the happy stars:
And so when my time comes to die, and I've got ary friend
'At wants expressed my last request I'll, mebby, rickommend
To drive slow, ef they haf to, goin' 'long the out'ard track,
But I'll smile and say, "You speed 'em
When the
Hearse
Comes
Back!"

OUR OLD FRIEND NEVERFAIL

O it's good to ketch a relative 'at's richer and don't run
When you holler out to hold up, and'll joke and have his fun;
It's good to hear a man called bad and then find out he's not,
Er strike some chap they call lukewarm 'at's really red-hot;
It's good to know the Devil's painted jes' a leetle black,
And it's good to have most anybody pat you on the back;
But jes' the best thing in the world's our old friend Neverfail,
When he wags yer hand as honest as an old dog wags his tail!

I like to strike the man I owe the same time I can pay,
And take back things I've borried, and su'prise folks thataway;
I like to find out that the man I voted fer last fall,
That didn't git elected, was a scoundrel after all;
I like the man that likes the pore and he'ps 'em when he can;
I like to meet a ragged tramp 'at's still a gentleman;
But most I like, with you, my boy, our old friend Neverfail,
When he wags yer hand as honest as an old dog wags his tail!

DAN O'SULLIVAN

Dan O'Sullivan: It's your
Lips have kissed "The Blarney," sure!
To be trillin' praise av me,
Dhrippin' shwate wid poethry!
Not that I'd not have ye sing
Don't lave off for anything
Jusht be aisy whilst the fit
Av me head shwells up to it!

Dade and thrue, I'm not the man,
Whilst yer singin', loike ye can,
To cry shtop because ye've blesht
My songs more than all the resht:
I'll not be the b'y to ax
Any shtar to wane or wax,
Or ax any clock that's woun',
To run up inshtid av down!

Whist yez! Dan O'Sullivan!
Him that made the Irishman
Mixt the birds in wid the dough,
And the dew and mistletoe
Wid the whusky in the quare
Muggs av us and here we air,
Three parts right, and three parts wrong,
Shpiked wid beauty, wit, and song!

JOHN BOYLE O'REILLY – SEPULTURE - BOSTON, AUGUST 13, 1890
Dead? this peerless man of men
Patriot, Poet, Citizen!
Dead? and ye weep where he lies
Mute, with folded eyes!

Courage! All his tears are done;
Mark him, dauntless, face the sun!
He hath led you. Still, as true,
He is leading you.

Folded eyes and folded hands
Typify divine commands
He is hearkening to, intent
Beyond wonderment.

'Tis promotion that has come
Thus upon him. Stricken dumb
Be your moanings dolorous!
God knows what He does.

Rather as your chief, aspire!
Rise and seize his toppling lyre,
And sing Freedom, Home, and Love,
And the rights thereof!

Ere in selfish grief ye sink,
Come! catch rapturous breath and think
Think what sweep of wing hath he,
Loosed in endless liberty.

MEREDITH NICHOLSON

Keats, and Kirk White, David Gray and the rest of you
Heavened and blest of you young singers gone,
Slender in sooth though the theme unexpressed of you,
Leave us this like of you yet to sing on!
Let your Muse mother him and your souls brother him,
Even as now, or in fancy, you do:
Still let him sing to us ever, and bring to us
Musical musings of glory and you.

Never a note to do evil or wrong to us
Beauty of melody, beauty of words,
Sweet and yet strong to us comes his young song to us
Rippled along to us clear as the bird's.
No fame elating him falsely, nor sating him
Feasting and fêting him faint of her joys,
But singing on where the laurels are waiting him,
Young yet in art, and his heart yet a boy's.

GOD'S MERCY

Behold, one faith endureth still
Let factions rail and creeds contend
God's mercy was, and is, and will
Be with us, foe and friend.

CHRISTMAS GREETING

A word of Godspeed and good cheer
To all on earth or far or near,
Or friend or foe, or thine or mine
In echo of the voice divine,
Heard when the Star bloomed forth and lit
The world's face, with God's smile on it.

TO RUDYARD KIPLING

To do some worthy deed of charity
In secret and then have it found out by
Sheer accident, held gentle Elia
That, that was the best thing beneath the sky!
Confirmed in part, yet somewhat differing
(Grant that his gracious wraith will pardon me
If impious!) I think a better thing
Is: being found out when one strives to be.

So, Poet and Romancer, old as young,
And wise as artless, masterful as mild,
If there be sweet in any song I've sung,
'Twas savored for that palate, O my Child!
For thee the lisping of the children all
For thee the youthful voices of old years
For thee all chords untamed or musical
For thee the laughter, and for thee the tears.

And thus, borne to me o'er the seas between
Thy land and mine, thy Song of certain wing
Circles above me in the "pure serene"
Of our high heaven's vast o'er-welcoming;
While, packeted with joy and thankfulness,
And fair hopes many as the stars that shine,
And bearing all love's loyal messages,
Mine own goes homing back to thee and thine.

THE GUDEWIFE

My gudewife, she that is tae be
O she sall seeme sang-sweete tae me
As her ain croon tuned wi' the chiel's
Or spinnin'-wheel's.
An' faire she'll be, an' saft, an' light,
An' muslin-bright
As her spick apron, jimpy laced
The-round her waiste.
Yet aye as rosy sall she bloome
Intil the roome
(The where alike baith bake an' dine)
As a full-fine
Ripe rose, lang rinset wi' the raine,
Sun-kist againe,
Sall seate me at her table-spread,
White as her bread.
Where I, sae kissen her for grace,
Sall see her face
Smudged, yet aye sweeter, for the bit
O' floure on it,
Whiles, witless, she sall sip wi' me
Luve's tapmaist-bubblin' ecstasy.

TENNYSON - ENGLAND, OCTOBER 5, 1892

We of the New World clasp hands with the Old
In newer fervor and with firmer hold
And nobler fellowship,

O Master Singer, with the finger-tip
Of Death laid thus on thy melodious lip!

All ages thou has honored with thine art,
And ages yet unborn thou wilt be part
Of all songs pure and true!
Thine now the universal homage due
From Old and New World ay, and still The New!

ROSAMOND C. BAILEY

Thou brave, good woman! Loved of every one;
Not only that in singing thou didst fill
Our thirsty hearts with sweetness, trill on trill,
Even as a wild bird singing in the sun
Not only that in all thy carols none
But held some tincturing of tears to thrill
Our gentler natures, and to quicken still
Our human sympathies; but thou hast won
Our equal love and reverence because
That thou wast ever mindful of the poor,
And thou wast ever faithful to thy friends.
So, loving, serving all, thy best applause
Thy requiem the vast throng at the door
Of the old church, with mute prayers and amens.

MRS. BENJAMIN HARRISON - WASHINGTON, OCTOBER 25, 1892

Now utter calm and rest;
Hands folded o'er the breast
In peace the placidest,
All trials past;
All fever soothed all pain
Annulled in heart and brain,
Never to vex again
She sleeps at last.

She sleeps; but O most dear
And best beloved of her
Ye sleep not nay, nor stir,
Save but to bow
The closer each to each,
With sobs and broken speech,
That all in vain beseech
Her answer now.

And lo! we weep with you,
One grief the wide world through:
Yet with the faith she knew

We see her still,
Even as here she stood
All that was pure and good
And sweet in womanhood
God's will her will.

GEORGE A. CARR - GREENFIELD, JULY 21, 1914

O playmate of the far-away
And dear delights of Boyhood's day,
And friend and comrade true and tried
Through length of years of life beside,
I bid you thus a fond farewell
Too deep for words or tears to tell.

But though I lose you, nevermore
To greet you at the open door,
To grasp your hand or see your smile,
I shall be thankful all the while
Because your love and loyalty
Have made a happier world for me.

So rest you, Playmate, in that land
Still hidden from us by His hand,
Where you may know again in truth
All of the glad days of your youth
As when in days of endless ease
We played beneath the apple trees.

TO ELIZABETH - OBIT JULY 8, 1893

O noble, true and pure and lovable
As thine own blessed name, ELIZABETH!
Ay, even as its cadence lingereth
Upon the lips that speak it, so the spell
Of thy sweet memory shall ever dwell
As music in our hearts. Smiling at Death
As on some later guest that tarrieth,
Too gratefully o'erjoyed to say farewell,
Thou hast turned from us but a little space
We miss thy presence but a little while,
Thy voice of sympathy, thy word of cheer,
The radiant glory of thine eyes and face,
The glad midsummer morning of thy smile,
For still we feel and know that thou art here.

TO ALMON KEEFER - INSCRIBED IN "TALES OF THE OCEAN"

This first book that I ever knew
Was read aloud to me by you!
Friend of my boyhood, therefore take
It back from me, for old times' sake
The selfsame "Tales" first read to me,
Under "the old sweet apple tree,"
Ere I myself could read such great
Big words, but listening all elate,
At your interpreting, until
Brain, heart, and soul were all athrill
With wonder, awe, and sheer excess
Of wildest childish happiness.

So take the book again, forget
All else, long years, lost hopes, regret;
Sighs for the joys we ne'er attain,
Prayers we have lifted all in vain;
Tears for the faces seen no more,
Once as the roses at the door!
Take the enchanted book. And lo,
On grassy swards of long ago,
Sprawl out again, beneath the shade
The breezy old-home orchard made,
The veriest barefoot boy indeed
And I will listen as you read.

TO - "THE J. W. R. LITERARY CLUB"

Well, it's enough to turn his head to have a feller's name
Swiped with a Literary Club! But you're the ones to blame!
I call the World to witness that I never agged ye to it
By ever writin' Classic-like because I couldn't do it:
I never run to "Hellicon," ner writ about "Per-nassus,"
Ner ever tried to rack or ride around on old "P-gassus"!
When "Tuneful Nines" has cross'd my lines, the ink 'ud blot and blur it,
And pen 'ud jest putt back fer home, and take the short way fer it!
And so, as I'm a-sayin', when you name your Literary
In honor o' this name o' mine, it's railly nessessary
Whilse I'm a-thankin' you and all to warn you, ef you do it,
I'll haf to jine the thing myse'f 'fore I can live up to it!

LITTLE MAID-O'-DREAMS

Little Maid-o'-Dreams, with your
Eery eyes so clear and pure
Gazing, where we fain would see
Into far futurity,
Tell us what you there behold,
In your visions manifold!

What is on beyond our sight,
Biding till the morrow's light,
Fairer than we see to-day,
As our dull eyes only may?

Little Maid-o'-Dreams, with face
Like as in some woodland place
Lifts a lily, chaste and white,
From the shadow to the light;
Tell us, by your subtler glance,
What strange sorcery enchants
You as now, here, yet afar
As the realms of moon and star?
Have you magic lamp and ring,
And genii for vassaling?

Little Maid-o'-Dreams, confess
You're divine and nothing less,
For with mortal palms, we fear,
Yet must pet you, dreaming here
Yearning, too, to lift the tips
Of your fingers to our lips;
Fearful still you may rebel,
High and heav'nly oracle!
Thus, though all unmeet our kiss,
Pardon this! and this! and this!

Little Maid-o'-Dreams, we call
Truce and favor, knowing all!
All your magic is, in truth,
Pure foresight and faith of youth
You're a child, yet even so,
You're a sage, in embryo
Prescient poet, artist, great
As your dreams anticipate.
Trusting God and Man, you do
Just as Heaven inspires you to.

TO THE BOY WITH A COUNTRY - DAN WALLINGFORD

Dan Wallingford, my jo Dan!
Though but a child in years,
Your patriot spirit thrills the land
And wakens it to cheers,
You lift the flag, you roll the drums
We hear the bugle blow,
Till all our hearts are one with yours,
Dan Wallingford, my jo!

CLAUDE MATTHEWS - GOVERNOR OF INDIANA

Steadfastly from his childhood's earliest hour
From simplest country life to state and power
His worth has known advancement, each new height
A newer glory in his fellow's sight.

So yet his happy fate, though mute the breath
Of thronging multitudes and thundrous cheers,
Faith sees him raised still higher, through our tears,
By this divine promotion of his death.

TO LESLEY

Burns sang of bonny Lesley
As she gaed o'er the border,
Gaed like vain Alexander,
To spread her conquests farther.

I sing another Lesley,
Wee girlie, more alluring,
Who stays at home, the wise one,
Her conquests there securing.

A queen, too, is my Lesley,
And gracious, though blood-royal,
My heart her throne, her kingdom,
And I a subject loyal.

Long shall you reign, my Lesley,
My pet, my darling dearie,
For love, oh, little sweetheart,
Grows never old or weary.

THE JUDKINS PAPERS

FATHER AND SON

Mr. Judkins' boy came home yesterday with a bottle of bugs in his pocket, and as the quiet little fellow sat on the back porch in his favorite position, his legs elbowed and flattened out beneath him like a letter "W," his genial and eccentric father came suddenly upon him.

"And what's the blame' boy up to now?" said Mr. Judkins, in an assumed tone of querulous displeasure, as he bent over the boy from behind and gently tweaked his ear.

"Oh, here, mister!" said the boy, without looking up; "you thist let up on that, will you!"

"What you got there, I tell you!" continued the smiling Mr. Judkins, in a still gruffer tone, relinquishing the boy's ear, and gazing down upon the fluffy towhead with more than ordinary admiration. "What you got there?"

"Bugs," said the boy "you know!"

"Dead, are they?" said Mr. Judkins.

"Some of 'em's dead," said the boy, carefully running a needle through the back of a large bumblebee. "All these uns is, you kin bet! You don't think a feller 'ud try to string a live bumblebee, I reckon?"

"Well, no, 'Squire," said Mr. Judkins, airily, addressing the boy by one of the dozen nicknames he had given him; "not a live bumblebee, a real stem-winder, of course not. But what in the name o' limpin' Lazarus air you stringin' 'em fer?"

"Got a live snake-feeder," said the boy, ignoring the parental inquiry. "See him down there in the bottom, 'ith all th' other uns on top of him. Thist watch him now, an' you kin see him pant. I kin. Yes, an' I got a beetle 'at's purt' nigh alive, too, on'y he can't pull in his other wings. See 'em?" continued the boy, with growing enthusiasm, twirling the big-mouthed bottle like a kaleidoscope. "Hate beetles! 'cause they allus act so big, an' make s'much fuss about theirselves, an' don't know nothin' neither! Bet ef I had as many wings as a beetle I wouldn't let no boy my size knock the stuffin' out o' me with no bunch o' weeds, like I done him!"

"Howd'ye know you wouldn't?" said Mr. Judkins, austerely, biting his nails and winking archly to himself.

"W'y, I know I wouldn't," said the boy, "'cause I'd keep up in the air where I could fly, an' wouldn't come low down ut all, bumpin' around 'mongst them bushes, an' buzzin' against things, an' buttin' my brains out a-tryin' to git thue fence cracks."

"'Spect you'd ruther be a snake-feeder, wouldn't you, Bud?" said Mr. Judkins suggestively. "Snake-feeders has got about enough wings to suit you, ef you want more'n one pair, and ever' day's a picnic with a snake-feeder, you know. Nothin' to do but jes' loaf up and down the crick, and roost on reeds and cat-tails, er fool around a feller's fish-line and light on the cork and bob up and down with it till she goes clean under, don't you know?"

"Don't want to be no snake-feeder, neither," said the boy, "'cause they gits gobbled up, first thing they know, by these 'ere big green bullfrogs ut they can't ever tell from the skum till they've lit right in their mouth and then they're goners! No, sir;" continued the boy, drawing an extra quinine-bottle from another pocket, and holding it up admiringly before his father's eyes: "There's the feller in there ut I'd ruther be than have a pony!"

"W'y, it's a nasty p'izen spider!" exclaimed Mr. Judkins, pushing back the bottle with affected abhorrence, "and he's alive, too!"

"You bet he's alive!" said the boy, "an' you kin bet he'll never come to no harm while I own him!" and as the little fellow spoke his face glowed with positive affection, and the twinkle of his eyes, as he continued, seemed wonderfully like his father's own. "Tell you, I like spiders! Spiders is awful fat, all but their head and that's level, you kin bet! Flies hain't got no business with a spider. Ef a spider ever reaches fer a fly, he's his meat! The spider, he likes to loaf an' lay around in the shade an' wait fer flies an' bugs an' things to come a-foolin' round his place. He lays back in the hole in the corner of his web, an' waits till somepin' lights on it an' nen when he hears 'em buzzin', he thist crawls out an' fixes 'em so's they can't buzz, an' he's got the truck to do it with! I bet ef you'd unwind all the web-stuff out of thist one little spider not bigger'n a pill, it 'ud be long enough fer a kite-string! Onc't they wuz one in our wood-house, an' a taterbug got stuck in his web, an' the spider worked purt' nigh two days 'fore he got him so's he couldn't move. Nen he couldn't eat him neither, 'cause they's shells on 'em, you know, an' the spider didn't know how to hull him. Ever' time I'd go there the spider, he'd be a-wrappin' more stuff around th' ole bug, an' stoopin' down like he wuz a-whisperin' to him. An' one day I went in ag'in, an' he was a-hangin', alas an' cold in death! An' I poked him with a splinter an' his web broke off, 'spect he'd used it all up on the wicked bug, an' it killed him; an' I buried him in a' ink-bottle an' mashed the old bug 'ith a chip!"

"Yes," said Judkins, in a horrified tone, turning away to conceal the real zest and enjoyment his face must have betrayed; "yes, and some day you'll come home p'izened, er somepin'! And I want to say right here, my young man, ef ever you do, and it don't kill you, I'll lint you within an inch of your life!" And as the eccentric Mr. Judkins whirled around the corner of the porch he heard the boy murmur in his low, absent-minded way, "Yes, you will!"

MR. JUDKINS' REMARKS
Judkins stopped us in front of the post-office yesterday to say that that boy of his was "the blamedest boy outside o' the annals o' history!" "Talk about this boy-naturalist out here at Indianapolis," says Judkins, "w'y, he ain't nowhere to my boy! The little cuss don't do nothin' either only set around and look sleepy, and dern him, he gits off more dry things than you could print in your paper. Of late he's been a-displayin' a sort o' weakness fer Nature, don't you know; and he's allus got a bottle o' bugs in his pocket. He come home yesterday evening with a blame' mud-turtle as big as an unabridged dictionary, and turned him over in the back yard and commenced biffin' away at him with a hammer and a cold-chisel. 'W'y, you're a-killin' the turtle,' says I. 'Kill nothin'!' says he, 'I'm thist a-takin' the lid off so's I can see his clock works.' Hoomh!" says Judkins: "He's a good one! only," he added, "I wouldn't have the boy think so fer the world!"

JUDKINS' BOY ON THE MUD-TURTLE
The mud-turtle is not a beast of pray, but he dearly loves catfish bait. If a mud-turtle gits your big toe in his mouth he will hang on till it thunders. Then he will spit it out like he was disgusted. The mud-turtle kin swim and keep his chin out of water ef he wants to but he don't care ef he does sink. The turtle kin stay under water until his next birthday, an' never crack a smile. He kin breathe like a grown person, but he don't haf to, on'y when he is on dry land, an' then I guess he thist does it to be soshibul. Allus when you see bubbles a-comin' up in the swimmin' hole, you kin bet your galluses they's a mud-turtle a-layin' down there, studyin' up some cheap way to git his dinner. Mud-turtles never dies, on'y when they make soup out of 'em. They is seven kinds of meat in the turtle, but I'd ruther eat thist plain burnt liver.

ON FROGS
Frogs is the people's friend, but they can't fly. Onc't they wuz tadpoles about as big as lickerish drops, an' after while legs growed on 'em. Oh, let us love the frog, he looks so sorry. Frogs kin swim better'n little boys, and they don't haf to hold their nose when they dive, neither. Onc't I had a pet frog; an' the cars run over him. It thist squshed him. Bet he never knowed what hurt him! Onc't they wuz a rich lady swallered one, when he wuz little, you know; an' he growed up in her, an' it didn't kill him ut all. An' you could hear him holler in her bosom. It was a tree-toad; and so ever' time he'd go

p-r-r-r-r- w'y, nen the grand lady she'd know it was goin' to rain, an' make her little boy run an' putt the tub under the spout. Wasn't that a b'utiful frog?

ON PIRUTS

Piruts is reckless to a fault. They ain't afeard of nobody ner nothin'. Ef ever you insult a pirut onc't, he'll foller you to the grave but what he will revenge his wrongs. Piruts all looks like pictures of "Buffalo Bill", on'y they don't shave off the whiskers that sticks out over the collar of their low-necked shirt. Ever' day is a picknick fer the piruts of the high seas. They eat gunpowder an' drink blood to make 'em savage, and then they kill people all day, an' set up all night an' tell ghost stories an' sing songs such as mortal ear would quail to listen to. Piruts never comes on shore on'y when they run out of tobacker; an' then it's a cold day ef they don't land at midnight, an' disguize theirselves an' slip up in town like a sleuth houn', so's the Grand Jury can't git on to 'em. They don't care fer the police any more than us people who dwells right in their midst. Piruts makes big wages an' spends it like a king. "Come easy, go easy," is the fatal watchword of them whose deeds is Deth. Onc't they wuz a pirut turned out of the house an' home by his cruel parents when he wuz but a kid, an' so he always went by that name. He was thrust adrift without a nickel, an' sailed fer distant shores to hide his shame fer those he loved. In the dead of night he stol'd a new suit of the captain's clothes. An' when he growed up big enough to fit 'em, he gaily dressed hissef and went up an' paced the quarter-deck in deep thought. He had not fergot how the captain onc't had lashed him to the jib-boom-poop an' whipped him. That stung his proud spirit even then; an' so the first thing he done was to slip up behind the cruel officer an' push him over-board. Then the ship wuz his fer better er fer worse. An' so he took command, an' hung high upon the beetling mast the pirut flag. Then he took the Bible his old mother give him, an' tied a darnic round it an' sunk it in the sand with a mocking laugh. Then it wuz that he wuz ready fer the pirut's wild seafaring life. He worked the business fer all they wuz in it fer many years, but wuz run in ut last. An', standin' on the gallus-tree, he sung a song which wuz all wrote off by hissef. An' then they knocked the trap on him. An' thus the brave man died and never made a kick. In life he wuz allus careful with his means, an' saved up vast welth, which he dug holes and buried, an' died with the secret locked in his bosom to this day.

ON HACKMENS

Hackmens has the softest thing in the bizness. They hain't got nothin' to do but look hump-shouldered an' chaw tobacker an' wait. Hackmens all looks like detectives, an' keeps still, an' never even spits when you walk past 'em. An' they're allus cold. A hackman that stands high in the p'fession kin wear a overcoat in dog-days an' then look chilly an' like his folks wuz all dead but the old man, an' he wuz a drunkard. Ef a hackman would on'y be a blind fiddler he'd take in more money than a fair-ground. Hackmens never gives nothin' away. You kin trust a hackman when you can't trust your own mother. Some people thinks when they hire a hack to take 'em some place that the hackman has got some grudge ag'in' 'em, but he hain't, he's allus that way. He loves you but he knows his place, and smothers his real feelings. In life's giddy scenes hackmens all wears a mask; but down deep in their heart you kin bet they are yourn till deth. Some hackmens look like they wuz stuck up, but they hain't, it's only 'cause they got on so much clothes. Onc't a hackman wuz stabbed by a friend of his in the same bizness, an' when the doctors wuz seein' how bad he wuz karved up, they found he had on five shurts. They said that wuz all that saved his life. They said ef he'd on'y had on four shurts, he'd 'a' been a ded man. An' the hackman hissef, when he got well, used to brag it wuz the closetest call he ever had, an' laid fer the other hackman, an' hit him with a car couplin' an' killed him, an' come mighty nigh goin' to the penitenchary fer it. Influenshal friends wuz all that saved him that time. No five shurts would 'a' done it. The mayor said that when he let him off, an' brought down the house, an' made hissef a strong man fer another term. Some mayors is purty slick, but a humble hackman may sometimes turn out to be thist as smooth. The on'y thing w'y a hackman don't show up no better is 'cause he loses so much sleep. That's why he allus looks like he had the headache, an' didn't care ef he did. Onc't a hackman wuz waitin' in front of a hotel one morning an' wuz sort o' dozin' like, an' fell off his seat. An' they run an' picked him up, an' he wuz unconshus, an' they worked with him till 'way long in the afternoon 'fore they found out he wuz thist asleep; an' he cussed fearful cause they waked him up, an' wondered why people couldn't never tend to their own bizness like he did.

ON DUDES

Ever'body is allus a-givin' it to Dudes. Newspapers makes fun of 'em, an' artists makes pictures of 'em; an' the on'y ones in the wide world that stuck on Dudes is me an' the Dudes theirse'f, an' we love an' cherish 'em with all a parent's fond regards. An' nobody knows much about Dudes neither, 'cause they hain't been broke out long enough yit to tell thist what the disease is. Some say it's softinning of the brains, an' others claim it can't be that, on the groun's they hain't got material fer the softinning to work on, &c., &c., till even "Sientests is puzzled," as the good book says. An' ef I wuz a-goin' to say what ails Dudes I'd have to give it up, er pernounce it a' aggervated case of Tyfoid blues, which is my 'onnest convictions. That's what makes me kind o' stand in with 'em, same as ef they wuz the under-dog. I am willing to aknolege that Dudes has their weakness, but so has ever'thing. Even Oscar Wild, ef putt to the test; an' I allus feel sorry fer George Washington 'cause he died 'fore he got to see Oscar Wild. An' then another reason w'y you oughten't to jump on to Dudes is, they don't know what's the matter with 'em any more than us folks in whom they come in daily contack. Dudes all walks an' looks in the face like they wuz on their way to fill an engagement with a revolvin' lady wax-figger in some milliner-winder, an' had fergot the number of her place of bizness. Some folks is mean enough to bitterly a'sert that Dudes is strained in their manner an' fools from choice; but they ain't. It's a gift, Dudes is Geenuses, that's what Dudes is!

ON RED HAIR

Onc't a pore boy wuz red-hedded, an' got mad at the other boys when they'd throw it up to him. An' when they'd laugh at his red hed, an' ast him fer a light, er wuzn't he afeard he'd singe his cap, an' orto' wear a tin hat, er pertend to warm their hands by him, w'y, sometimes the red-hedded boy'd git purty hot indeed; an' onc't he told another boy that wuz a-bafflin' him about his red hair that ef he wuz him he'd git a fine comb an' go to canvassin' his own hed, and then he'd be liabul to sceer up a more livelier subjeck to talk about than red hair. An' then the other boy says, "You're a liar" an' that got the red-hedded boy into more trouble; fer the old man whipped him shameful' fer breakin' up soil with the other boy. An' this here red-hedded boy had freckles, too. An' warts. An' nobody ortn't to 'a' jumpt on to him fer that. Ef anybody wuz a red-hedded boy they'd have also warts an' freckles, an' thist red-hair's bad enough. Onc't another boy told him ef he wuz him he bet he could make a big day look sick some night. An' when the red-hedded boy says "How?" w'y, the other boy he says "Easy enough. I'd thist march around bare-hedded in the torch-light p'cession." - "Yes, you would," says the red-hedded boy, an' pasted him one with a shinny club, an' got dispelled from school 'cause he wuz so high-tempered an' impulsiv. Ef I wuz the red-hedded boy I'd be a pirut; but he allus said he wuz goin' to be a baker.

THE CROSS-EYED GIRL

"You don't want to never tamper with a cross-eyed girl," said Mr. Judkins, "and I'll tell you w'y: They've natur'lly got a better focus on things than a man would ever guess, studyin' their eyes, you understand. A man may think he's a-foolin' a cross-eyed girl simply because she's apparently got her eyes tangled on other topics as he's a-talkin' to her, but at the same time that girl may be a-lookin' down the windin' stairway of the cellar of his soul with one eye, and a-winkin' in a whisper to her own soul with the other, and her unconscious victim jes' a-takin' it fer granted that nothin' is the matter with the girl, only jes' cross-eyes! You see I've studied 'em," continued Judkins, "and I'm on to one fact dead sure, and that is, their natures is as deceivin' as their eyes is! Knowed one onc't that had her eyes mixed up thataway, sensitive little thing she was, and always referrin' to her 'misfortune,' as she called it, and eternally threatenin' to have some surgeon straighten 'em out like other folks', and, sir, that girl so worked on my feelin's, and took such underholts on my sympathies that, blame me, before I knowed it I confessed to her that ef it hadn't 'a' been fer her defective eyes (I made it 'defective') I never would have thought of lovin' her, and, furthermore ef ever she did have 'em changed back normal, don't you understand, she might consider our engagement at an end, I did, honest. And that girl was so absolute cross-eyed it warped her ears, and she used to amuse herself by watchin' 'em curl up as I'd be a-talkin' to her, and that maddened me, 'cause I'm natur'lly of a jealous disposition, you know, and so, at last, I jes' casually hinted that ef she was really a-goin' to git them eyes carpentered up, w'y she'd better git at it: and that ended it.

"And then the blame' girl turned right around and married a fellow that had a better pair of eyes than mine this minute! Then I struck another cross-eyed girl, not really a legitimate case, 'cause, in reality, she only had one off eye, the right eye, ef I don't disremember, the other one was as square as a gouge. And that girl was, ef any difference, a more confusin' case than the other, and besides all that, she had some money in her own right, and warn't a-throwin' off no big discount on one game eye. But I finally got her interested, and I reckon something serious might 'a' come of it, but, you see, her father was dead, and her stepmother sort o' shet down on my comin' to the house; besides that, she had three grown uncles, and you know how uncles is. I didn't want to marry no family, of course, and so I slid out of the scheme, and tackled a poor girl that clerked in a post-office. Her eyes was bad! I never did git the hang of them eyes of hern. She had purty hair, and a complexion, I used to tell her, which outrivalled the rose. But them eyes, you know! I didn't really appreciate how bad they was crossed, at first. You see, it took time. Got her to give me her picture, and I used to cipher on that, but finally worked her off on a young friend of mine who wanted to marry intellect, give her a good send-off to him, and she was smart, only them eyes, you know! Why, that girl could read a postal card, both sides at once, and smile at a personal friend through the office window at the same time!"

HOMESICKNESS
There was a more than ordinary earnestness in the tone of Mr. Judkins as he said: "Referrin' to this thing of bein' homesick, I want to say right here that of all diseases, afflictions er complaints, this thing of bein' homesick takes the cookies! A man may think when he's got a' aggrivated case of janders, er white-swellin', say, er bone-erysipelas, that he's to be looked up to as bein' purty well fixed in this vale of trouble and unrest, but I want to tell you, when I want my sorrow blood-raw, don't you understand, you may give me homesickness, straight goods, you know, and I'll git more clean, legitimate agony out of that than you can out of either of the other attractions, yes, er even ef you'd ring in the full combination on me! You see, there's no way of treatin' homesickness only one, and that is to git back home, but as that's a remedy you can't git at no drug store, at so much per box, and ef you could, fer instance, and only had enough ready money anyhow to cover half the cost of a full box, and nothin' but a full box ever reached the case, w'y, it follers that your condition still remains critical. And homesickness don't show no favors. It's jes' as liable to strike you as me. High er low, er rich er poor, all comes under her jurisdiction, and whenever she once reaches fer a citizen, you can jes' bet she gits there Eli, ever' time!

"She don't confine herse'f to youth, ner make no specialty of little children either, but she stalks abroad like a census-taker, and is as conscientious. She visits the city girl clean up to Maxinkuckee, and makes her wonder how things really is back home without her. And then she haunts her dreams, and wakes her up at all hours of the night, and sings old songs over fer her, and talks to her in low thrillin' tones of a young man whose salary ain't near big enough fer two; and then she leaves her photograph with her and comes away, and makes it lively fer the boys on the train, the conductor, the brakeman and the engineer. She even nests out the travellin' man, and yanks him out of his reclinin' chair, and walks him up and down the car, and runs him clean out of cigars and finecut, and smiles to hear him swear. Then she gits off at little country stations and touches up the night operator, who grumbles at his boy companion, and wishes to dernation 'six' was in, so's he could 'pound his ear.'

"And I'll never forget," continued Mr. Judkins, "the last case of homesickness I had, and the cure I took fer it. 'Tain't been more'n a week ago neither. You see my old home is a'most too many laps from this base to make it very often, and in consequence I hadn't been there fer five years and better, till this last trip, when I jes' succumbed to the pressure, and th'owed up my hands and went. Seemed like I'd 'a' died if I hadn't. And it was glorious to rack around the old town again, things lookin' jes' the same, mighty nigh, as they was when I was a boy, don't you know. Run acrost an old schoolmate, too, and tuck supper at his happy little home, and then we got us a good nickel cigar, and walked and walked, and talked and talked! Tuck me all around, you understand, in the meller twilight, till, the first thing you know, there stood the old schoolhouse where me and him first learnt to chew tobacco, and all that! Well, sir! you hain't got no idea of the feelin's that was mine! W'y, I felt like I could th'ow my arms around the dear old buildin' and squeeze it till the cupolo would jes' pop out of the top of the roof like the core out of a b'ile! And I think if they ever was a' epoch in my life when I could 'a' tackled poetry without no compunctions, as the feller says, w'y, then was the time shore!"

TO THE QUIET OBSERVER - ERASMUS WILSON, AFTER HIS LONG SILENCE
Dear old friend of us all in need
Who know the worth of a friend indeed,
How rejoiced are we all to learn
Of your glad return.

We who have missed your voice so long
Even as March might miss the song
Of the sugar-bird in the maples when
They're tapped again.

Even as the memory of these
Blended sweets, the sap of the trees
And the song of the birds, and the old camp too,
We think of you.

Hail to you, then, with welcomes deep
As grateful hearts may laugh or weep!
You give us not only the bird that sings,
But all good things.

AMERICA'S THANKSGIVING - 1900
Father all bountiful, in mercy bear

With this our universal voice of prayer
The voice that needs must be
Upraised in thanks to Thee,
O Father, from Thy Children everywhere.

A multitudinous voice, wherein we fain
Wouldst have Thee hear no lightest sob of pain
No murmur of distress,
Nor moan of loneliness,
Nor drip of tears, though soft as summer rain.

And, Father, give us first to comprehend,
No ill can come from Thee; lean Thou and lend
Us clearer sight to see
Our boundless debt to Thee,
Since all thy deeds are blessings, in the end.

And let us feel and know that, being Thine,
We are inheritors of hearts divine,
And hands endowed with skill,
And strength to work Thy will,
And fashion to fulfilment Thy design.

So, let us thank Thee, with all self aside,
Nor any lingering taint of mortal pride;
As here to Thee we dare
Uplift our faltering prayer,
Lend it some fervor of the glorified.

We thank Thee that our land is loved of Thee
The blessèd home of thrift and industry,
With ever-open door
Of welcome to the poor
Thy shielding hand o'er all abidingly.

Even thus we thank Thee for the wrong that grew
Into a right that heroes battled to,
With brothers long estranged,
Once more as brothers ranged
Beneath the red and white and starry blue.

Ay, thanks though tremulous the thanks expressed
Thanks for the battle at its worst, and best
For all the clanging fray
Whose discord dies away
Into a pastoral song of peace and rest.

WILLIAM PINKNEY FISHBACK
Say first he loved the dear home-hearts, and then

He loved his honest fellow citizen
He loved and honored him, in any post
Of duty where he served mankind the most.

All that he asked of him in humblest need
Was but to find him striving to succeed;
All that he asked of him in highest place
Was justice to the lowliest of his race.

When he found these conditions, proved and tried,
He owned he marvelled, but was satisfied
Relaxed in vigilance enough to smile
And, with his own wit, flay himself a while.

Often he liked real anger as, perchance,
The summer skies like storm-clouds and the glance
Of lightning for the clearer, purer blue
Of heaven, and the greener old earth, too.

All easy things to do he did with care,
Knowing the very common danger there;
In noblest conquest of supreme debate
The facts are simple as the victory great.

That which had been a task to hardiest minds
To him was as a pleasure, such as finds
The captive-truant, doomed to read throughout
The one lone book he really cares about.

Study revived him: Howsoever dim
And deep the problem, 'twas a joy to him
To solve it wholly; and he seemed as one
Refreshed and rested as the work was done.

And he had gathered, from all wealth of lore
That time has written, such a treasure store,
His mind held opulence, his speech the rare
Fair grace of sharing all his riches there

Sharing with all, but with the greatest zest
Sharing with those who seemed the neediest:
The young he ever favored; and through these
Shall he live longest in men's memories.

JOHN CLARK RIDPATH
To the lorn ones who loved him first and best,
And knew his dear love at its tenderest,
We seem akin, we simplest friends who knew
His fellowship, of heart and spirit too:

We who have known the happy summertide
Of his ingenuous nature, glorified
With the inspiring smile that ever lit
The earnest face and kindly strength of it:

His presence, all-commanding, as his thought
Into unconscious eloquence was wrought,
Until the utterance became a spell
That awed us as a spoken miracle.

Learning, to him, was native, was, in truth,
The earliest playmate of his lisping youth,
Likewise, throughout a life of toil and stress,
It was as laughter, health and happiness:

And so he played with it, joyed at its call
Ran rioting with it, forgetting all
Delights of childhood, and of age and fame,
A devotee of learning, still the same!

In fancy, even now we catch the glance
Of the rapt eye and radiant countenance,
As when his discourse, like a woodland stream,
Flowed musically on from theme to theme:

The skies, the stars, the mountains, and the sea,
He worshipped as their high divinity
Nor did his reverent spirit find one thing
On earth too lowly for his worshipping.

The weed, the rose, the wildwood or the plain,
The teeming harvest, or the blighted grain
All, all were fashioned beautiful and good,
As the soul saw and senses understood.

Thus broadly based, his spacious faith and love
Enfolded all below as all above
Nay, ev'n if overmuch he loved mankind,
He gave his love's vast largess as designed.

Therefore, in fondest, faithful service, he
Wrought ever bravely for humanity
Stood, first of heroes for the Right allied
Foes, even, grieving, when (for them) he died.

This was the man we loved are loving yet,
And still shall love while longing eyes are wet
With selfish tears that well were brushed away
Remembering his smile of yesterday.

For, even as we knew him, smiling still,
Somewhere beyond all earthly ache or ill,
He waits with the old welcome, just as when
We met him smiling, we shall meet again.

NEW YEAR'S NURSERY JINGLE

Of all the rhymes of all the climes
Of where and when and how,
We best and most can boost and boast
The Golden Age of NOW!

TO THE MOTHER

The mother-hands no further toil may know;
The mother-eyes smile not on you and me;
The mother-heart is stilled, alas! But O
The mother-love abides eternally.

TO MY SISTER - A BELATED OFFERING FOR HER BIRTHDAY

These books you find three weeks behind
Your honored anniversary
Make me, I fear, to here appear
Mayhap a trifle cursory.
Yet while the Muse must thus refuse
The chords that fall caressfully,
She seems to stir the publisher
And dealer quite successfully.

As to our birthdays let 'em run
Until they whir and whiz!
Read Robert Louis Stevenson,
And hum these lines of his:
"The eternal dawn, beyond a doubt,
Shall break on hill and plain
And put all stars and candles out
Ere we be young again."

A MOTTO

The Brightest Star's the modestest,
And more'n likely writes
His motto like the lightnin'-bug's
Accordin' To His Lights.

TO A POET ON HIS MARRIAGE - MADISON CAWEIN

Ever and ever, on and on,
From winter dusk to April dawn,
This old enchanted world we range
From night to light, from change to change
Or path of burs or lily-bells,
We walk a world of miracles.

The morning evermore must be
A newer, purer mystery
The dewy grasses, or the bloom
Of orchards, or the wood's perfume
Of wild sweet-williams, or the wet
Blent scent of loam and violet.

How wondrous all the ways we fare
What marvels wait us, unaware!...
But yesterday, with eyes ablur
And heart that held no hope of Her,
You paced the lone path, but the true
That led to where she waited you.

ART AND POETRY - TO HOMER C. DAVENPORT

"Wess," he says, and sort o' grins,
"Art and Poetry is twins.
'F I could draw as you have drew,
Like to jes' swap pens with you."

HER SMILE OF CHEER AND VOICE OF SONG - ANNA HARRIS RANDALL

Spring fails, in all its bravery of brilliant gold and green,
The sun, the grass, the leafing tree, and all the dazzling scene
Of dewy morning orchard blooms,
And woodland blossoms and perfumes
With bird-songs sown between.

Yea, since she smiles not any more, so every flowery thing
Fades, and the birds seem brooding o'er her silence as they sing
Her smile of cheer and voice of song
Seemed so divinely to belong
To ever-joyous Spring!

Nay, still she smiles. Our eyes are blurred and see not through our tears:
And still her rapturous voice is heard, though not of mortal ears:
Now ever doth she smile and sing
Where Heaven's unending clime of Spring
Reclaims those gifts of hers.

Old Indiany, 'course we know
Is first, and best, and most, also,
Of all the States' whole forty-four:
She's first in ever'thing, that's shore!
And best in ever'way as yet
Made known to man; and you kin bet
She's most, because she won't confess
She ever was, or will be, less!
And yet, fer all her proud array
Of sons, how many gits away!
No doubt about her bein' great
But, fellers, she's a leaky State!
And them that boasts the most about
Her, them's the ones that's dribbled out.
Law! jes' to think of all you boys
'Way over here in Illinoise
A-celebratin', like ye air,
Old Indiany, 'way back there
In the dark ages, so to speak,
A-prayin' for ye once a week
And wonderin' what's a-keepin' you
From comin', like you ort to do.
You're all a-lookin' well, and like
You wasn't "sidin' up the pike,"
As the tramp-shoemaker said
When "he sacked the boss and shed
The blame town, to hunt fer one
Where they didn't work fer fun!"
Lookin' extry well, I'd say,
Your old home so fur away.
Maybe, though, like the old jour.,
Fun hain't all yer workin' fer.
So you've found a job that pays
Better than in them old days
You was on The Weekly Press,
Heppin' run things, more er less;
Er a-learnin' telegraph
Operatin', with a half
Notion of the tinner's trade,
Er the dusty man's that laid
Out designs on marble and
Hacked out little lambs by hand,
And chewed fine-cut as he wrought,
"Shapin' from his bitter thought"
Some squshed mutterings to say,
"Yes, hard work, and porer pay!"
Er you'd kind o' thought the far-

Gazin' kuss that owned a car
And took pictures in it, had
Jes' the snap you wanted bad!
And you even wondered why
He kep' foolin' with his sky-
Light the same on shiny days
As when rainin'. ('T leaked always.)
Wondered what strange things was hid
In there when he shet the door
And smelt like a burnt drug store
Next some orchard-trees, i swan!
With whole roasted apples on!
That's why Ade is, here of late,
Buyin' in the dear old State,
So's to cut it up in plots
Of both town and country lots.

ABE MARTIN

Abe Martin! dad-burn his old picture!
P'tends he's a Brown County fixture
A kind of a comical mixture
Of hoss-sense and no sense at all!
His mouth, like his pipe, 's allus goin',
And his thoughts, like his whiskers, is flowin',
And what he don't know ain't wuth knowin'
From Genesis clean to baseball!

The artist, Kin Hubbard, 's so keerless
He draws Abe most eyeless and earless,
But he's never yet pictured him cheerless
Er with fun 'at he tries to conceal,
Whuther onto the fence er clean over
A-rootin' up ragweed er clover,
Skeert stiff at some "Rambler" er "Rover"
Er newfangled automobeel!

It's a purty steep climate old Brown's in;
And the rains there his ducks nearly drowns in
The old man hisse'f wades his rounds in
As ca'm and serene, mighty nigh
As the old handsaw-hawg, er the mottled
Milch cow, er the old rooster wattled
Like the mumps had him 'most so well throttled
That it was a pleasure to die.

But best of 'em all's the fool-breaks 'at
Abe don't see at all, and yit makes 'at
Both me and you lays back and shakes at
His comic, miraculous cracks

Which makes him clean back of the power
Of genius itse'f in its flower
This Notable Man of the Hour,
Abe Martin, The Joker on Facts.

O. HENRY - WRITTEN IN THE CHARACTER OF "SHERRARD PLUMMER"
O. Henry, Afrite-chef of all delight!
Of all delectables conglomerate
That stay the starved brain and rejuvenate
The mental man. Th' esthetic appetite
So long anhungered that its "in'ards" fight
And growl gutwise, its pangs thou dost abate
And all so amiably alleviate,
Joy pats its belly as a hobo might
Who haply hath attained a cherry pie
With no burnt bottom in it, ner no seeds
Nothin' but crispest crust, and thickness fit,
And squshin'-juicy, and jes' mighty nigh
Too dratted drippin'-sweet fer human needs,
But fer the sosh of milk that goes with it.

"MONA MACHREE"
"Mona Machree, I'm the wanderin' cr'ature now,
Over the sea;
Slave of no lass, but a lover of Nature now
Careless and free."
- T. A. Daly.

Mona Machree! och, the sootherin' flow of it,
Soft as the sea,
Yet, in-under the mild, moves the wild undertow of it
Tuggin' at me,
Until both the head and the heart o' me's fightin'
For breath, nigh a death all so grandly invitin'
That barrin' your own livin' yet I'd delight in,
Drowned in the deeps of this billowy song to you
Sung by a lover your beauty has banned,
Not alone from your love but his dear native land,
Whilst the kiss of his lips, and touch of his hand,
And his song all belong to you,
Mona Machree!

WILLIAM McKINLEY - CANTON, OHIO, SEPTEMBER 30, 1907
He said: "It is God's way:
His will, not ours be done."

And o'er our land a shadow lay
That darkened all the sun.
The voice of jubilee
That gladdened all the air,
Fell sudden to a quavering key
Of suppliance and prayer.

He was our chief, our guide
Sprung of our common Earth,
From youth's long struggle proved and tried
To manhood's highest worth:
Through toil, he knew all needs
Of all his toiling kind
The favored striver who succeeds
The one who falls behind.

The boy's young faith he still
Retained through years mature
The faith to labor, hand and will,
Nor doubt the harvest sure
The harvest of man's love
A nation's joy that swells
To heights of Song, or deeps whereof
But sacred silence tells.

To him his Country seemed
Even as a Mother, where
He rested, slept; and once he dreamed
As on her bosom there
And thrilled to hear, within
That dream of her, the call
Of bugles and the clang and din
Of war.... And o'er it all

His rapt eyes caught the bright
Old Banner, winging wild
And beck'ning him, as to the fight ...
When even as a child
He wakened. And the dream
Was real! And he leapt
As led the proud Flag through a gleam
Of tears the Mother wept.

His was a tender hand
Even as a woman's is
And yet as fixed, in Right's command,
As this bronze hand of his:
This was the Soldier brave
This was the Victor fair
This is the Hero Heaven gave
To glory here and There.

As tangible a form in History
The Spirit of this man stands forth as here
He towers in deathless sculpture, high and clear
Against the bright sky of his destiny.
Sprung of our oldest, noblest ancestry,
His pride of birth, as lofty as sincere,
Held kith and kin, as Country, ever dear
Such was his sacred faith in you and me.
Thus, natively, from youth his work was one
Unselfish service in behalf of all
Home, friends, and sharers of his toil and stress;
Ay, loving all men and despising none,
And swift to answer every righteous call,
His life was one long deed of worthiness.

The voice of Duty's faintest whisper found
Him as alert as at her battle-cry
When awful War's battalions thundered by,
High o'er the havoc still he heard the sound
Of mothers' prayers and pleadings all around;
And ever the despairing sob and sigh
Of stricken wives and orphan children's cry
Made all our Land thrice consecrated ground.
So rang his "Forward!" and so swept his sword
On! on! till from the fire-and-cloud once more
Our proud Flag lifted in the glad sunlight
As though the very Ensign of the Lord
Unfurled in token that the strife was o'er,
And victory, as ever, with the right.

LEE O. HARRIS - CHRISTMAS DAY - 1909
O say not he is dead,
The friend we honored so;
Lift up a grateful voice instead
And say: He lives, we know
We know it by the light
Of his enduring love
Of honor, valor, truth, and right,
And man, and God above.

Remember how he drew
The child-heart to his own,
And taught the parable anew,
And reaped as he had sown;
Remember with what cheer

He filled the little lives,
And stayed the sob and dried the tear
With mirth that still survives.

All duties to his kind
It was his joy to fill;
With nature gentle and refined,
Yet dauntless soul and will,
He met the trying need
Of every troublous call,
Yet high and clear and glad indeed
He sung above it all.

Ay, listen! Still we hear
The patriot song, the lay
Of love, the woodland note so dear
These will not die away.
Then say not he is dead,
The friend we honor so,
But lift a grateful voice instead
And say: He lives, we know.

THE HIGHEST GOOD - WRITTEN FOR A HIGH-SCHOOL ANNUAL

To attain the highest good
Of true man and womanhood,
Simply do your honest best
God with joy will do the rest.

MY CONSCIENCE

Sometimes my Conscience says, says he,
"Don't you know me?"
And I, says I, skeered through and through,
"Of course I do.
You air a nice chap ever' way,
I'm here to say!
You make me cry, you make me pray,
And all them good things thataway
That is, at night. Where do you stay
Durin' the day?"

And then my Conscience says, onc't more,
"You know me shore?"
"Oh, yes," says I, a-trimblin' faint,
"You're jes' a saint!
Your ways is all so holy-right,
I love you better ever' night
You come around, tel' plum daylight,

When you air out o' sight!"

And then my Conscience sort o' grits
His teeth, and spits
On his two hands and grabs, of course,
Some old remorse,
And beats me with the big butt-end
O' that thing tel my clostest friend
'Ud hardly know me. "Now," says he,
"Be keerful as you'd orto be
And allus think o' me!"

MY BOY

You smile and you smoke your cigar, my boy;
You walk with a languid swing;
You tinkle and tune your guitar, my boy,
And you lift up your voice and sing;
The midnight moon is a friend of yours,
And a serenade your joy
And it's only an age like mine that cures
A trouble like yours, my boy!

THE OBJECT LESSON

Barely a year ago I attended the Friday afternoon exercises of a country school. My mission there, as I remember, was to refresh my mind with such material as might be gathered, for a "valedictory," which, I regret to say, was to be handed down to posterity under another signature than my own.

There was present, among a host of visitors, a pale young man of perhaps thirty years, with a tall head and bulging brow and a highly intellectual pair of eyes and spectacles. He wore his hair without roach or "part" and the smile he beamed about him was "a joy forever." He was an educator, from the East, I think I heard it rumoured, anyway he was introduced to the school at last, and he bowed, and smiled, and beamed upon us all, and entertained us after the most delightfully edifying manner imaginable. And although I may fail to reproduce the exact substance of his remarks upon that highly important occasion, I think I can at least present his theme in all its coherency of detail. Addressing more particularly the primary department of the school, he said:

"As the little exercise I am about to introduce is of recent origin, and the bright, intelligent faces of the pupils before me seem rife with eager and expectant interest, it will be well for me, perhaps, to offer by way of preparatory preface, a few terse words of explanation.

"The Object Lesson is designed to fill a long-felt want, and is destined, as I think, to revolutionize, in a great degree, the educational systems of our land. In my belief, the Object Lesson will supply a want which I may safely say has heretofore left the most egregious and palpable traces of mental confusion and intellectual inadequacies stamped, as it were, upon the gleaming reasons of the most learned, the highest cultured, and the most eminently gifted and promising of our professors and scientists both at home and abroad.

"Now this deficiency, if it may be so termed, plainly has a beginning; and probing deeply with the bright, clean scalpel of experience we discover that, 'As the twig is bent the tree's inclined.' To remedy, then, a deeply seated error which for so long has rankled at the very root of educational progress throughout the land, many plausible, and we must admit, many helpful theories have been introduced to allay the painful errors resulting from the discrepancy of which we speak: but until now, nothing that seemed wholly to eradicate the defect has been discovered, and that, too, strange as it may seem, is, at last, emanating, like the mighty river, from the simplest source, but broadening and gathering in force and power as it flows along, until, at last, its grand and mighty current sweeps on in majesty to the vast illimitable ocean of, of, of - Success! Ahem!

"And, now, little boys and girls, that we have had by implication, a clear and comprehensive explanation of the Object Lesson and its mission, I trust you will give me your undivided attention while I endeavor, in my humble way, to direct your newly acquired knowledge through the proper channel. For instance:

"This little object I hold in my hand, who will designate it by its proper name? Come, now, let us see who will be the first to answer. 'A peanut,' says the little boy here at my right. Very good, very good! I hold, then, in my hand, a peanut. And now who will tell me, what is the peanut? A very simple question, who will answer? 'Something good to eat,' says the little girl. Yes, 'something good to eat,' but would it not be better to say simply that the peanut is an edible? I think so, yes. The peanut, then, is an edible, now, all together, an edible!

"To what kingdom does the peanut belong? The animal, vegetable, or mineral kingdom? A very easy question. Come, let us have prompt answers. 'The animal kingdom,' does the little boy say? Oh, no! The peanut does not belong to the animal kingdom! Surely the little boy must be thinking of a larger object than the peanut, the elephant, perhaps. To what kingdom, then, does the peanut belong? The v-v-veg, 'The vegetable kingdom,' says the bright-faced little girl on the back seat. Ah! that is better. We find then that the peanut belongs to the, what kingdom? The 'vegetable kingdom.' Very good, very good!

"And now who will tell us of what the peanut is composed. Let us have quick responses now. Time is fleeting! Of what is the peanut composed? 'The hull and the goody,' some one answers. Yes, 'the hull and the goody' in vulgar parlance, but how much better it would be to say simply, the shell and the kernel. Would not that sound better? Yes, I thought you would agree with me there!

"And now who will tell me the color of the peanut! And be careful now! for I shouldn't like to hear you make the very stupid blunder I once heard a little boy make in reply to the same question. Would you like to hear what color the stupid little boy said the peanut was? You would, eh? Well, now, how many of you would like to hear what color the stupid little boy said the peanut was? Come now, let's have an expression. All who would like to hear what color the stupid little boy said the peanut was, may hold up their right hands. Very good, very good, there, that will do.

"Well, it was during a professional visit I was once called upon to make to a neighboring city, where I was invited to address the children of a free school. Hands down, now, little boy, founded for the exclusive benefit of the little newsboys and bootblacks, who, it seems, had not the means to defray the expenses of the commonest educational accessories, and during an object lessen, identical with the one before us now, for it is a favorite one of mine, I propounded the question, what is the color of the peanut? Many answers were given in response, but none as sufficiently succinct and apropos as I deemed the facts demanded; and so at last I personally addressed a ragged, but, as I then thought, a bright-eyed little fellow, when judge of my surprise, in reply to my question what is the color of the peanut, the little fellow, without the slightest gleam of intelligence lighting up his face, answered, that 'if not scorched in roasting, the peanut was a blond.' Why, I was almost tempted to join in the general merriment his inapposite reply elicited. But I occupy your attention with trivial things; and as I notice the time allotted to me has slipped away, we will drop the peanut for the present. Trusting the few facts gleaned from a topic so homely and unpromising will sink deep in your minds, in time to bloom and blossom in the fields of future usefulness, I, I, I thank you."

James Whitcomb Riley – A Short Biography

Poet and author James Whitcomb Riley was born on October 7th 1849 in Greenfield, Indiana. Known as the "Hoosier Poet" for his work with regional dialects, and as the "Children's Poet" for his children's poetry and devotion to youth causes, Riley is best remembered as the author of the well-loved verse book, *Rhymes of Childhood.*

Riley grew up in a well-off and influential family. Riley's father, Reuben Andrew Riley, was a lawyer and Democrat member of the Indiana House of Representatives and he named his son for his friend James Whitcomb, then the governor of Indiana.

Riley had a spotty education, learning at home and attending his local school sporadically (he did not graduate Grade 8 until the age of twenty). Nonetheless, his was a childhood full of creativity. He learned about poetry from an uncle who was a poet and enthusiast and was encouraged by his mother to write and produce juvenile theatrical presentations. His father taught him how to play the guitar and Riley went on to perform in a local band.

Life changed when Riley's father went off to fight in the Civil War in 1861. The family (which already included six children) took in an additional orphan child and suffered many hardships. Riley would base his famous poem, *Little Orphant Annie* on this temporary foster sibling (both the child and the poem were named "Allie", but a typesetter made a crucial typo when the poem was finally published).

Riley Senior returned from soldiering a broken man, partially paralyzed and unable to resume his practice. The family was forced to sell their house in town and retreated to the family farm where Riley's mother died in 1870. Riley became estranged from his father at this time and left home. He also started drinking excessively, beginning a life-long habit that would both impact his health and his career.

He embarked on a series of low-paying jobs – house painting, Bible salesman – before starting a sign-painting business in Greenfield. Riley wrote catchy slogans for his signs, in effect, his first published verses. He also started participating in local theatre productions and sending poems to the *Indianapolis Mirror* under the pseudonym "Jay Whit".

When he went to work for the McGrillus Company in Anderson, Indiana shilling tonic medicines in a travelling show that visited small towns around the state, he discovered another calling. Riley both wrote and performed skits promoting the tonics. Eventually, Riley and several friends started a billboard company that became successful enough that he was able to turn to writing in a more committed way, and he returned to Greenfield to do so.

Riley started sending out dozens of poems to newspapers around the country and many of them – the *Danbury News*, the *Indianapolis Journal* and the *Anderson Democrat*, among them – published the verses. At the same time, Riley began to write to prominent American writers, sending poems and requesting their endorsement. He was successful with poet Henry Wadsworth Longfellow who wrote back, "I have read the poems with great pleasure, and I think they show a true poetic faculty and insight." Riley would finally meet Longfellow in person shortly before the latter's death in 1882; he famously wrote about the experience and about Longfellow's profound impact on his work.

The *Anderson Democrat* offered Riley a reporting job in 1877. He took it on while continuing to submit poems at journals and newspapers all over the country. Riley would lose the stability of this reporting job when a prank in which he submitted a poem to a journal claiming it was Edgar Allan Poe's went awry. Spurned by many publishers after this embarrassing incident, Riley joined a travelling lecture circuit and gave poetry readings around the state. A born entertainer, Riley's readings would become hugely popular and remained a primary source of income for most of his life.

Eventually, the Poe debacle faded into the background and the *Indianapolis Journal* relented, hiring Riley as a columnist in 1879; he wrote regularly for them about society affairs while continuing to tour his increasingly theatrical and comedic poetry readings. As his fame increased, Riley dropped his "Jay Whit" pseudonym and wrote under his own name from about 1881.

Around this time Riley began writing what are known as his "Boone County poems". They are almost entirely written in dialect and emphasize rural and agricultural topics, often evoking nostalgia for the simplicity of country life. *The Old Swimmin'-Hole* and *When the Frost Is on the Punkin'* were the most popular, and helped earn the entire series critical acclaim. In 1883, a friend arranged for the private publication of *The Old Swimmin' Hole and 'Leven More Poems'*. The book's popularity dictated a second printing before the end of the year and it continued to sell for years, bolstered by Riley's reading tours.

Riley's prose style lent itself well to public performance. With their emphasis on the natural speech rhythms of mid-western dialects, his most famous poems – *Raggedy Man*, *Little Orphant Annie* – can look slightly ridiculous on the page. But they come alive when read aloud:

Little Orphant Annie's come to our house to stay,
An' wash the cups an' saucers up, an' brush the crumbs away,
An' shoo the chickens off the porch, an' dust the hearth, an'sweep,
An' make the fire, an' bake the bread, an' earn her board-an'-keep;
An' all us other childern, when the supper-things is done,
We set around the kitchen fire an' has the mostest fun
A-list'nin' to the witch-tales 'at Annie tells about,
An' the Gobble-uns 'at gits you
Ef you
Don't
Watch
Out!

This phenomenon is likely the key to Riley's success with children's verse, as well as the reason he was able to build such fame and fortune on the travelling lecture circuit. It helped also that he was a confident and talented performer.

In 1881 Riley was invited to tour with the Redpath Lyceum Circuit, a prominent series that included writers such as Ralph Waldo Emerson on its roster of regular lecturers. After a successful first season reading in Chicago and Indianapolis, Riley signed a ten-year contract with the Circuit and embarked on a tour of the Eastern seaboard starting in Boston. Riley toured with the Circuit until 1885 when he joined forces with humourist Edgar Wilson Nye. In 1888, the pair co-wrote *Nye and Riley's Railway Guide*, a collection of poems and anecdotes. Nye and Riley also teamed up with another famous American humourist Samuel Clemons (Mark Twain) for joint performances in New York City. Despite contract and agent woes that deprived Riley of his full share of the proceeds, he continued touring with Nye through 1890.

Riley published his third compilation of work in 1888. *Old-Fashioned Roses* was written specifically for the British market and consisted mostly of sonnets; Riley intentionally left his country bumpkin dialects out of this collection. The book was a predictable success in the UK and Riley travelled to Scotland (where he made a pilgrimage to the grave of Robert Burns, a poet with who he is often compared) and England to promote it and conduct readings in 1891.

Back home the next year Riley resumed his lecture and reading tour, teaming up with millionaire author Douglass Sherley for a hugely successful double bill. Coinciding with this, in a savvy and astute cross-promotion, Riley compiled and published perhaps his best-loved book, *Rhymes of Childhood*. It's a work that continues to be popular into the 21st century. It also parted the beginning of the end for Riley's literary reputation. Although he continued to sell out readings in New York and across the US (in fact prospective audience members were often turned away), critics increasingly found his work repetitive and banal. His 1894 verse volume *Armazindy* was very poorly received.

Riley gave his last tour in 1895 and spent his final years in Indianapolis writing patriotic poetry for public recitation on civic occasions (with stirring titles such as *America!* and *The Name of Old Glory*) and poem/elegies for famous friends. His life's work of essays, poems, plays and articles was published in sixteen volumes in 1914.

By this time, Riley was in poor health, weakened by years of heavy drinking. The Hoosier Poet died on July 23, 1916 of a stroke. In a final, unusual tribute, Riley lay in state for a day in the Indiana Statehouse, where thousands came to pay their respects. Not since Lincoln had a public personage received such a send-off. He is buried at Crown Hill Cemetery in Indianapolis.

Riley's legacy is not just a literary one. A wealthy man, he left behind the funding seeds for a number of memorial projects, the James Whitcomb Riley Hospital for Children, Camp Riley for children with disabilities and James Whitcomb Riley House (a museum in which the writer's personal effects and furnishings from his lifetime remain unchanged).

And, as a lasting tribute, the town of Greenfield holds a festival every year in Riley's honor. Every October the "Riley Days" festival opens with a flower parade in which local school children place flowers around the statue of Riley set on the courthouse lawn.

Remembered as both a philanthropist and a poet laureate for the Hoosier state of Indiana, a writer with a distinctive pre-industrial folk ethos and an ear for the humble rhythms of the plain local dialect of the US Midwest, Riley remains to this day a poet of the people.